The Eight Masks of Men
A Practical Guide in Spiritual Growth for Men of the Christian Faith

THE HAWORTH PASTORAL PRESS
Pastoral Care, Ministry, and Spirituality
Richard Dayringer, ThD
Senior Editor

New, Recent, and Forthcoming Titles:

A Memoir of a Pastoral Counseling Practice by Robert L. Menz

When Life Meets Death: Stories of Death and Dying, Truth and Courage by Thomas W. Shane

The Heart of Pastoral Counseling: Healing Through Relationship, Revised Edition by Richard Dayringer

The Eight Masks of Men: A Practical Guide in Spiritual Growth for Men of the Christian Faith by Frederick G. Grosse

Hidden Addictions: A Pastoral Response to the Abuse of Legal Drugs by Bridget Clare McKeever

Rev. Frederick G. Grosse, DMin

The Eight Masks of Men
A Practical Guide in Spiritual Growth for Men of the Christian Faith

Pre-publication
REVIEWS,
COMMENTARIES,
EVALUATIONS . . .

"**I**n his introduction to *The Eight Masks of Men: A Practical Guide in Spiritual Growth for Men of the Christian Faith*, Dr. Frederick Grosse states that with this book he hopes to 'ring the bell buried in our souls.' I believe his book has great potential for doing that for many men and women. Although specifically aimed at men's spiritual growth, the book will certainly have a favorable impact on women and on families of men who read it and take it to heart. Dr. Grosse lays out a nine-week program that, if followed as designed, would give men a powerful initiation into what I consider to be the best outcome of the 'men's movement' of the late 1980s and 1990s—that is, ongoing intimate groups of men who truly nurture and support one another emotionally and spiritually. I have been a member of a men's group myself for over ten years and it has had a profound impact on each of the members' lives. The men's groups, if they function optimally, do remove the masks that Dr. Grosse so clearly discusses, leading to transformations in men's lives. The special emphasis that Dr. Grosse has added to the basic thrust of such groups is the focus on Christian spirituality that seeks to ground those transformations in Christian theology and the broader Christian community.

I found this to be an excellent book for men who are seeking ways to break through some of the barriers that limit their lives emotionally and spiritually. It distills some of the best achievements of the men's movement over the past decade and applies that learning in a Christian context. It reinforces the need for community and provides very useful, practical ways to go about creating and strengthening Christian community. I highly recommend its use in churches and seminaries as a tool for spiritual growth."

Timothy A. Sanderson, MD
Jungian Analyst;
Assistant Professor of Clinical
Psychiatry and Behavioral Sciences,
Eastern Virginia Medical School,
Norfolk, VA

"**F**red Grosse has written a book that is thoroughly grounded in traditional Christian spirituality and that is thoughtfully aware of the needs of men in our culture. He has wisely put the two together in a way that serves the needs of no other agenda than that of the spiritual development of human beings. His approach embodies the standards that ought to always be applied in what is too often an area of shallow trendiness. Close attention to what he points us to could make men's groups once again a vital spiritual force in the church."

Eric O. Springsted, PhD
Chaplain and Professor
of Philosophy and Religion,
Illinois College,
Jacksonville, IL

"**M**uch has been published about the 'men's movement' already. However, almost all of it has been in a secular vein. Fred Grosse has written a book on the men's movement from a theological point of view. It is practical and describes a repeatable organization and content for a men's group in any church. The theology that can undergird such a men's group is included in a thorough way. Churches that provide a men's group can utilize this book to enable spiritual growth in the Christian faith."

Rev. Richard Dayringer, ThD
Professor Emeritus,
School of Medicine,
Southern Illinois University
Springfield, IL

"**A**s an ordained Pastor I am always looking for books that will be helpful, especially in the spiritual area. This book is not only helpful, but very practical. Grosse invites us beyond other books written about masculine spirituality. He welcomes us into the reality of where most men in the pew live. He dares to raise the questions that are there for men, but are rarely addressed. In this book Fred Grosse walks the talk. He shares his own story as a way of inviting us into our stories. His mask comes off so others may take off their masks.

Whether we are just beginning our spiritual exploration, or whether we have been exploring for many years, Fred speaks to us. The other thing he does is make it practical. I can hardly wait to try this book out in my own congregation. As a Pastor I don't have the time to create a program for group discussion. Grosse has done this for me. The program speaks to people where they are living spiritually. Try it, you may like it."

Pastor Gary G. Arndt
Richfield United Church of Christ;
Chair of the Spiritual Development
Network of the United Church of Christ,
Richfield, OH

The Eight Masks of Men
A Practical Guide in Spiritual Growth for Men of the Christian Faith

Rev. Frederick G. Grosse, DMin

The Haworth Pastoral Press
An Imprint of The Haworth Press, Inc.
New York • London

Published by

The Haworth Pastoral Press, an imprint of The Haworth Press, Inc., 10 Alice Street, Binghamton, NY 13904-1580

[Scripture quotations are] from the Revised Standard Version of the Bible, copyright 1946, 1952, 1971 by the Division of Christian Education of the National Council of the Churches of Christ in the USA. Used by permission.

Quoted material has been taken from the following works:

Wildmen, Warriors, and Kings by Patrick M. Arnold. © 1991 Crossroads Publishing Co., 370 Lexington Avenue, New York, NY. Used by permission.

The Collected Works of St. John of the Cross, translated by Kieran Kavanaugh and Otilio Rodriguez © 1979, 1991 by Washington Province of Discalced Carmelites, ICS Publications, 2131 Lincoln Road, NE, Washington, DC 20002-1199. USA.

Fire in the Belly by Sam Keen. © 1991. Used by permission of Bantam Books, a division of Bantam, Doubleday, Dell Publishing Group, Inc.

Knights Without Armor by Aaron R. Kipnis. © 1991 by Aaron R. Kipnis. Reprinted by permission of Jeremy P. Tarcher, Inc., a division of the Putnam Publishing Group.

Body Theology by James B. Nelson © 1992. Westminster/John Knox Press. Used by permission.

Cover design by Monica L. Seifert.

Library of Congress Cataloging-in-Publication Data

Grosse, Frederick G.
    The eight masks of men : a practical guide in spiritual growth for men of the Christian faith / Frederick G. Grosse.
        p.   cm.
    Includes bibliographical references and index.
    ISBN 0-7890-0416-X (alk. paper).
    1. Men—Religious life. 2. Men (Christian theology). I. Title.
BV4528.2.G76   1998
248.8'42—dc21
                                                                97-26363
                                                                    CIP

With appreciation
for the life and teachings of Juan de Yepes

ABOUT THE AUTHOR

Rev. Frederick G. Grosse, DMin, is President/CEO of Elon Homes for Children in Charlotte and Elon College, North Carolina, and is a leader in local, state, and national programs concerning Christian spiritual growth for men. He received his Doctor of Ministry degree from Boston University with a major in Religion, Culture, and Personality and a focus on Christian masculine spirituality. Reverend Grosse is an ordained minister and was a parish minister in Jacksonville, Illinois, and Virginia Beach, Virginia for twelve years.

CONTENTS

Foreword

While it is an exciting time to be a man in our society, it is also a very confusing one. Take John Wayne's image, for example. Whether we agreed with his portrayal of manhood or not, at least we thought *he* believed it. Even those who have abandoned this icon of American masculinity as an unhelpful image for our times have assumed that at least this man was who his movies said he was. Now we learn in Garry Wills' recent biography that John Wayne actually hated horses, liked suits and ties more than jeans, and had to remind himself to say "ain't." And though he called on generations to sacrifice their lives in wartime, he avoided military service during World War II.[1] As the Angel Gabriel in the movie *Green Pastures* told us, everything we thought was nailed down is coming loose!

But there are more serious reasons for our confusion about masculinity. For one, we men are still all too invisible to ourselves. For centuries men have assumed that they are "normative humanity," the standard by which all else is measured. Thus, Professor Higgins in *My Fair Lady* could sing, "Why can't a woman be more like a man?" With such assumptions, however, men have not been seriously motivated to explore their own distinctive experience as men. But, the costs of invisibility to ourselves are great. We wonder why we, more than women, are lonely, stressed, angry, sick, and die prematurely. The statistics do not lie. The causes are not male biology. The causes are gender constructions.

Thankfully, however, things are changing. For the past couple of decades, more and more men have been gathering in study groups, support groups, retreats, and conferences to plumb their own depths and their own hungers as men. This practical and eminently readable book by Frederick Grosse will be a highly useful tool for just such exploration. The author has keen insights into both the fears of the journey (hence, the masks we wear) and the deep hungers that lie beneath those masks. He is no bystander. He has been and is on that journey himself, and opens his life with vulnerability to the reader.

Another reason that this is a confusing time lies in the way that many men hear the critiques that some feminist women level at them. They hear women saying that men are by nature defective: competitive, violent, and unfeeling, unable to talk about anything other than sports and computers, and incapable of asking for directions when lost. Hearing these criticisms, some men get angry, others become defensive, and still others experience shame.

None of these responses are helpful for us or for anyone else, as Frederick Grosse well knows. And he knows well that men are not *inherently* prone to any of these things. The detachment from feelings, the competitiveness, the violence, and all of the other unhealthy qualities many men experience are not inborn. They are not part of the nature of the male sex. They are qualities of certain *masculinities*—which are socially created and learned gender roles. They have become masks. But what has been learned can be unlearned. What gender understandings have been socially created can be creatively transformed.

Because of the author's clarity about the important difference between *sex* (male) and *gender* (masculine)—the former given by God, the latter socially created and learned—he is both nondefensive and hopeful. Much in our gender learnings *has* been oppressive to us as men, as well as to women, children, and the natural world. We need not be defensive (and the author is not) when women or other men level critiques at some of our masculine ways of being in the world. The critics are allies for our health. The images of masculinity we that have taken for granted can be radically questioned. Thus, the author is hopeful, and I with him. In new ways of seeing ourselves, we men have an enormous amount to gain ourselves—as well as everyone and everything else on this fragile planet.

I celebrate this book also because it is frankly and solidly *theological.* There is much talk about "spirituality" these days. Some of that talk is very good, but some of it is rather vacuous and rootless. The helpful treatment of men's spirituality throughout this book is strongly rooted in biblical faith and Christian affirmations. The author knows the paradoxes of faith well—that in willingness to lose life one will find it; in committed discipline we find freedom; in facing our powerlessness there is a new kind of power. This is a masculine spirituality well grounded in our faith's tradition.

I particularly want to underscore Dr. Grosse's strong emphasis on grace throughout these pages. Grace is at the heart of the Christian gospel, but it is also the reality most difficult for men shaped by cultural masculinity to grasp and be grasped by. For those of us with years of conditioning toward going it alone, toward competing and winning, the word of grace can sound oddly foreign. For those of us who learned sexism and homophobia as part of being "a real man," grace is strange because it says we do not have to justify ourselves by putting other people down. In many ways, grace runs directly counter to much in cultural masculinity. Yet, it is that for which we most deeply hunger. And it is indispensable to our transformation and our fulfillment.

Finally, I want to challenge every man who uses this wise and practical book to see it as an important beginning. The focus here is on personal change. That is the author's intent, and it is compellingly and helpfully done. But "the personal is political," as the women's movement has rightly reminded us. Biblical faith, in which Frederick Grosse is immersed, knows that the transformed individual is also under the Great Commission—to go to the nations.

Thus, faithful men are interested not only in personal fulfillment, but in the good news of equality and justice. Over the ages men have made enormous contributions for the good of the world. Of that I have no doubt whatsoever. I am also convinced that the institutions of our common life are now groaning under the weight of distorted masculinities. The causes of racism, social violence, environmental abuse, and vast economic disparities are many and complex, of course. But distortions in masculinity are close to the center of these social ills.

So, the author's constant emphasis on community is important, indeed. Just as the church does not exist for itself but for the world, so also new men exist not simply for themselves (or even for their families or close relationships) but also for the realm of God.

I take renewed hope for the church and for the world when I see men serious about change. Dr. Grosse's book is an exciting and practical tool for that life-giving process.

James B. Nelson
Professor Emeritus of Christian Ethics
United Theological Seminary of the Twin Cities

NOTE

1. See Garry Wills, *John Wayne's America: The Politics of Celebrity* (New York: Simon & Schuster, 1997).

Preface

As a leader in local, state, and national programs concerning Christian spiritual growth for men, I have written this book as an answer to questions I have heard from men of varying religious and personal backgrounds from around the country. I am a forty-one-year-old male who has been involved in the men's movement in the community and the church for nine years, as an ordained minister of the United Church of Christ and, previously as a parish minister in Jacksonville, Illinois, and Virginia Beach, Virginia for twelve years. I was a member of an ongoing men's group that met weekly in Virginia Beach and is now in its seventh year. My doctoral thesis at Boston University School of Theology (1994) is centered upon the church's need to address the spiritual needs of men.

This is an excellent book for Christian men who are seeking a hands-on, practical guide in Christian spiritual growth. It offers, to the individual man, or to small communities of men, a nine-week program for growing in the Christian faith. Based in Scripture and informed by the men's movement literature today, this book presents a practical and deliberate guidebook for men. The text contains three chapters of background information on men's issues, such as: men's secrets and the harm they cause, the church's avoidance of male spirituality, men in American culture, why spirituality is difficult for men, a history of Christian spirituality, and thirteen disciplines of the Christian faith. These three chapters are followed by eight chapters that present the specific masks men wear that prevent them from living a more joyous and abundant life. Each of these eight chapters has biblical examples, contemporary metaphors, humor, and challenging information. At the end of each chapter is a list of ten questions to promote reflection and direction. These eight chapters offer what is unique and dynamic about this text. The chapters discuss the following topics: loneliness/solitude and community, rage and anger/pain and hurt, compulsions/love, performance/acceptance, control/friendship, producing/beingness, competition/humility, and institutional religion/spiritual growth.

This is an easy to read yet very challenging book for Christian men (or women who want to know more about men's spiritual needs), who seek practical guidance in faith growth. The book contains a healthy mixture of Bible accounts, Christian theology, spirituality, humor, and everyday experiences. This book provides excellent material for an existing men's church group or for men who are looking for guidance in forming a group centered upon Christian faith issues. The book concludes with a chapter offering advice on building a men's spirituality group (including liturgy) and with a chapter listing interesting men's stories in the Bible. This book provides a rare opportunity for men to learn how to remove the masks they have been wearing, in a safe and accepting environment, and to nurture the sacred gifts beneath them that God has given each man.

Chapter 1. Introduction: *Why You Need This Book*

This chapter suggests why men need to read this book. It includes the account of my near-death experience and how this transformed my life. It discusses why men need to seek union with God, the Ten Commandments of Patriarchy, covenants men have made today and the hurt these covenants may cause, and biblical accounts to highlight these issues. This chapter is designed to identify familiar but unspoken issues for men, and to pique men's interest in reading the book.

Chapter 2. Practical Use: *How to Use This Book*

Today's man typically wants to know how something can benefit him. While not trivializing the Christian faith, this chapter discusses what the book can do for the man in his everyday life. There are simply no other books available that present this type of practical information. The foundation for the eight masks and the thirteen Christian disciplines used to remove them are offered in this chapter. There is also some practical information on how to establish a good and safe men's group. This chapter contains the "guts" of what I have to offer that is unique and worthy on the ongoing conversation of men's Christian spiritual growth.

Chapter 3. Thirteen Christian Spiritual Disciplines

There are two focal points in this chapter: the life and teachings of St. John of the Cross, a Christian spiritualist, and an examination of the thirteen Christian spiritual disciplines. In St. John of the Cross, men are exposed to the rich and powerful gifts God has for those who struggle in the faith. There is an overview of St. John's life and his struggles as well as an emphasis on the active and passive parts of sensual and spiritual issues in the Christian tradition. The chapter then offers an individual summary of the thirteen Christian disciplines as revealed in Scripture. There is a biblical and a practical application for each. This is a very important chapter for any man considering Christian spiritual growth.

Chapter 4. The Mask of Loneliness Hides a Man's Desire for Community

This chapter focuses on a common situation for men—living with a sense of isolation and loneliness. It examines biblical and contemporary examples of loneliness. There is also an overview of messages in society that push men into loneliness. The text then offers examples of how men can remove this mask and celebrate the joys of solitude and community.

Chapter 5. The Mask of Rage and Anger Hides a Man's Pain and Hurt

Many men are poorly experienced at feeling or expressing pain and hurt. From a young age, many boys learn that these are unacceptable emotional and spiritual feelings in our society. To cover them up, men live with varying levels of rage and anger. This chapter examines why rage and anger can be productive doors to liberation in the expression of pain and hurt. The psychic and societal trauma this mask covers up is not to be underestimated.

Chapter 6. The Mask of Compulsions Hides a Man's Desire for Love

From the Tower of Babel until today, many men continue to "seek to make a name for themselves." They compulsively work, build, write, earn, risk, etc., day after day. Beneath this mask, however, is the hidden desire to love and be loved. Some men experience love, but many do not. Instead they lead compulsive, love-denying lives. Beneath the frenzy of these compulsions, this chapter explains, is the desire for love.

Chapter 7. The Mask of Performance Hides a Man's Desire for Acceptance

With little conscious thought, many men are driven by performance issues, not so much by what they produce in volume as by how well they are judged for what they do. Men continually perform in so many ways, and are usually rewarded or punished based upon their deeds, all at their own spiritual expense. Performance is an outward thrust; acceptance is an inward blessing. This chapter separates performance from acceptance and also looks at the issue of God's freely given grace.

Chapter 8. The Mask of Control Hides a Man's Desire for Friendship

One of the primary traits that has been given to the American male is control. Often, to be in control is viewed as manly, to be out of control or to be controlled is less than manly. One of the primary attributes of Christian spirituality is friendship. Friendship and control are very much opposed to each other. Behind the mask of control, many men are hungering for friendship—a friendship with other men, women, children, and Jesus Christ. This chapter looks at biblical and contemporary issues of control and friendship. Both of these issues are rarely discussed in the Christian church but nonetheless are powerful influences on a man's spirituality.

Chapter 9. The Mask of Producing Hides a Man's Desire to Just "Be"

Typically, a man is happiest when he is producing something. No matter what his vocation or avocation, this is an innate and societally reinforced part of being a man. However, when receiving the grace of God and the mercy of Jesus Christ, men are invited to just "be" and openly receive. To "be" is an active and a passive calling, as described in Chapter 3. This chapter includes information and an example of how the mask of producing can shield a man from the unmerited and unearned love of God.

Chapter 10. The Mask of Competition Hides a Man's Desire for Humility

From James and John seeking a special seat to current American business, sports, and even church settings, men compete. Freud may have located the genesis of this in castration anxiety, but we need to look deeper and more spiritually at the problem. Men seem to be natural-born competitors. They compete to out-do one another, to control one another, and to feel worthy. In the faith, however, Christ is calling them to humility, not competition. To surrender themselves to the will of God is very different than to compete with God. This chapter looks at the God-given desire to walk humbly in faith that is covered up by masks of competition.

Chapter 11. The Mask of Institutional Religion Hides a Man's Desire for Spiritual Growth

The institutional church can become a mask behind which men hide from true spiritual growth. Men fill pulpits, offices, and organizational functions, but are they growing in the faith? This chapter explores the very clear difference between church and spiritual-growth activities. There is an affirmation of the church here, but a caution not to let the institution become an end in and of itself. This chapter also covers the issue of why men are more prone to be "institutional" supporters instead of spiritual pilgrims.

Chapter 12. Conclusion and Suggestions

This chapter offers a conclusion that the masks must come off to reveal the God-given desires beneath them. The removal process is not instantaneous or easy, but it must be done to live the abundant life for which Jesus gave his life. Included in this chapter are some helpful suggestions for forming or reforming a men's church group, such as registration forms, evaluation forms, a code of conduct, and meeting and worship liturgy.

This book has been written for all men. It will certainly be most beneficial to Christian men in America. It is a text that women could read to appreciate mens' issues more keenly. This book is easily read by the average lay person of the church. It could also be an excellent text for undergraduate religion majors, seminary students, and students in training at Clinical Pastoral Education centers.

The text is a combination of scholarly review, biblical references, Christian tradition, contemporary story, humor and spiritual direction. There is no book on the market like it today.

—*Frederick D. Grosse, DMin*

Acknowledgments

Through this circle of friendship, I have experienced a community without masks: George, Mike, Robert, Gene, Bill, Kurt, and John.

With deepest appreciation I acknowledge my mentors, Elisha, Malcolm, John, Richard, Mike, and Kent.

For Suzanne and Katy, through whom the grace of God have shown me acceptance, forgiveness, hope, and, most of all, intimacy.

Special appreciation for my new life to: Gautum D. Desai, MD; David R. Dettaas, MD; and William P. Edmondson, MD.

In gratitude for the excellence in healing of children to the Board of Directors and staff of Elon Homes for Children.

Chapter 1

Introduction:
Why You Need This Book

This issues discussed in this book can affect your life and your relationships in a very positive way. I know this to be true because of a very powerful event in my own life.

On May 12, 1991, I was diagnosed by our family physician with "econococcal cystic disease of the liver." This is a very rare disease, and most frequently fatal. Through ultrasound and computerized tomography (CT scan) testing, physicians found three large septated cystic masses located within my liver. Each cyst was large and contained parasites. I showed no sign of such a serious illness except general flulike symptoms that had begun two days earlier. Because the disease was life threatening, I had to have surgery to remove the parasites and cysts. Prior to surgery, my wife and I were not given any sort of promise about the outcome due to the nature of the rare disease and the uncertainty of such extensive surgery involving the liver. The chances of my survival from the surgery and recovery period were quite unknown. During the eight-hour surgical procedure, the surgeons asperated the parasites and fluids out of each mass, sterilized the walls, and subsequently removed the cyst with a normal rim of liver tissue. A complete pericystectomy was subsequently performed shelling the pericyst membrane out from the liver bed. A postsurgical defect in the right lobe of my liver was then filled with omentum. My gallbladder was removed due to damage from the cystic growth. The three cystic masses, one each on the left and right lobe of my liver and one in the center below my sternum, also had to be surgically separated from my stomach, left diaphragm, spleen, pancreas, and right diaphragm. Following the surgery and seven-day hospitalization I was sent home for a seven-week period of recovery. While at home, I was given the drug Praziquantel for seven days as adjunctive medical therapy in case parasitic presence had spilled out of any cystic mass during surgery. Now, some four years later, I have the physical reminder of this life-and-death experience from a very obvious thirty-six-centimeter scar across my abdomen from the upper abdominal chevron incision. I have occasional stiffness and pain from the wound recovery area. I have no feeling on the surface of my skin throughout my abdominal area.

In his book *Body Theology*, James Nelson writes, ". . . body theology starts with the fleshy experience of life—with our hungers and our passions, our bodily aliveness and deadness . . . the task of body theology is critical reflection on our bodily experience as a fundamental realm of the experience of God."[1] My own personal experience is that Nelson is quite right. We experience God first and foremost through our bodies, for our body is truly who we are. As a result of this horrifying surgical event and near-death trauma, I have been directed by God to an awareness of my own spiritual hungers and needs. My body taught me how out of touch with it I was. My soul taught me how little I sought direction from God. My mind told me it is high time to put down my masks and seek the abundant life. This humbling event was a chilling awakening for me, an opportunity to look at the covenants I had made and to become aware of who I was listening to. I tell you this brief account so you can gather some appreciation for who is writing this book. I, too, am in the process of learning how to remove masks and seek direction from God. I have been humbled, converted, and transformed by surgery and will never go back to my prior way of living. To change one's lifestyle and spiritual endeavors does not come easily or overnight. It is a long, complex process which never ends. It is done with the help of God, and within the context of a supportive community. This is, indeed, the good news.

In the Bible we read, "Gracious is the Lord, and righteous: our God is merciful. The Lord preserves the simple: when I was low, God saved me. Return, O my soul, to your rest, for the Lord has dealt bountifully with you."[2] At a very intimate level, I experience these words. This entire chapter in the Psalms is a beautiful collection of verses that speak volumes to anyone who is ill or in need of

God's healing. Since God has allowed me to live, I have pondered my own spiritual activities and my life as a Christian man. This book is a response to what I have been learning. The past four years have been an exhilarating time for me to "move into" my body and explore the beauty God has created. It has been a time of seeking direction from God. It has been a time of building trusting and intimate relationships with other Christian men. It has been a time of meeting my family and friends anew, and developing more rich and life-sustaining relationships. It has become a season for me to practice the thirteen Christian spiritual disciplines and begin taking off my masks. Above all else, I have been given a time to savor my humility and to turn ashes of mourning into garlands of joy. I have experienced what it truly means to surrender to God, body, mind and spirit, and be saved. Like each of you, my faith is wholly impacted by my life's experiences. When St. John of the Cross wrote about the "dark night of the soul" (more about this in Chapter 3), he illumined for many of us a way through profound suffering to a place where we hear God calling our names. We who live so much by what we produce and how we look, who are too busy to meditate upon God's work, who use alcohol, sex, drugs, work, religion, hobbies, gossip, to deaden our anxieties and our pain, we who continually slave for that "something" that will make us feel complete, can truly give thanks when God takes everything away from us. For only then, when it is God and us, together, can we better prioritize and discipline our lives.

When we seek to remove our masks and receive spiritual growth, we are seeking change. We are seeking, or being sought after, for significant change in our lives. One night while I lay in the Virginia Beach General Hospital, there was a fairly severe thunderstorm coming across the Chesapeake Bay. I was laying in the bed directly next to the window. From there I could turn my head and see the thunderclouds moving toward land. I had a Foley catheter in my penis, a nasogastric tube in my nose and throat, and a needle in my back for pain medication. Because of the pain from surgery and my state of confusion and exhaustion, I could not move myself. Whenever I needed to be turned over or moved, several nurses had to do it.

The storm outside overshadowed the hospital. The lightning flashed everywhere, the rain pelted the windows, and the thunder shook the building. I was sure I was going to die. The electricity went out and emergency generators went on. Totally powerless to move or in any way help myself, I remember praying as strongly as I could for God to save me. Begging, really, *for God to unite with me as one.* I had recognized my own need to surrender to God for life. It was then, and is now, a time of spiritual transformation for me. There is no rational explanation for this, because I would not have been killed by the storm. But my belief was that I needed to *be in union with God at that moment, and forever, to survive.* All my masks came off in a hurry. Suddenly, and now over the years, the God-given desires beneath the masks I wore were exposed to the light of Christ. This was a spiritual moment I wish upon everyone, for it is miraculous. I do not wish you parasites or a thunderstorm, but a season of humility and surrender. A time to answer the voice that is calling your name. *A season of union with God.*

This release of control is very much the opposite of how most Christian men are raised and trained in our culture. Yet, to surrender the masks that separate us from God and humankind is the exact way to celebrate life in the faith. When we release our masks we are not vulnerable. We are standing, well protected, upon the rock of our salvation. There, the work of God will ring familiar in our souls. Whether we hear on the fourth or four-hundredth time, the Lord continues to call our names. When we listen, we release ourselves from our covenants of deception and we renew our true vow with our Creator. We no longer make covenants under clever ruse. We let go of the commandments of patriarchy and we put fresh light on the secrets we carry. This will lead us from loneliness and from fear to faith. Slowly or quickly, with illness or stillness, God does speak to us. God will leave us marked as Christ's own forever, a mark as sacred and as holy as our baptismal water and oil. The true task of spiritual growth is to remove our masks and seek union with the Lord—with God's help.

Many American men are trained from birth to be individualists and self-contained units of control. Nothing could be more detrimental to a union with God and the opposite of spiritual growth than this mind-set. So, our work is before us. This is no small task. In fact, to have spiritual needs and desires has been, until recently, just not "manly" in our country. The resulting premature death, ulcers, compulsions, addictions, unresolved anger and rage, fierce and reckless violence, child abandonment, and physical, verbal, and sexual abuses by males, are evidence enough that we need to redefine "manly." We need to help each other take off old patriarchal masks that are suffocating the Spirit within us. American men are in desperate need of ministry from the church. The myth of the lone male hero is just that, a myth. Men need community. Men need salvation from God, alone, and with other men who will love, support, challenge, encourage, and forgive them in noncompetitive, nonsexual ways. When Moses was in need, God gave him his brother, Aaron, to help. When David was fearful and fleeing Saul, Jonathan befriended him and their souls were "knitted together as one." When there was no room to get him through the doorway, the friends of the paralytic together lifted him to the rooftop. The Bible is instructive: men are in need, men are in want of healing, and men can help one another, with the love of God.

Much of the material in this book will ring a bell with the reader. This material will be familiar to you, whether you are new to men's spirituality work or a veteran at the effort. The purpose of this book is to help you clarify issues, organize your spiritual direction, become familiar again with the spiritual content of your own life story, and to appreciate the journey of other men. Far too often in our society men have become workhorses or intellectual beings or physical beings without regard for our emotional and spiritual well-being. What we shall endeavor to do with this book is to ring the bell buried in our souls. We want to move beneath jobs, power, status, tenure, titles, jealousy, envy, and strife to the core sense of our being, our souls. When we shed the masks we have been given or have put on ourselves and we make room for Christ in our souls, we will awaken with ringing clarity what is most familiar to us. An introspective life values ambiguity, contradictions, patience, and quiet. Men of the Judeo-Christian faith must embrace these values as well. This is mask-free living in the name of Jesus Christ. The true task of every Christian man is to reclaim the power and mystery of his baptismal covenant and to live every day with this covenant familiar to his soul. Then in our daily living, actions, beliefs, and relationships, our faith and trust in Jesus Christ will be shown.

We are not alone in our work of surrendering our masks. We get direction from God. Recall the story of the Israelite people and the battles at Jericho and Ai. Moses was not to make his way into the Promised Land with the people Israel. Joshua, son of Nun, would be their leader. So it came to pass and the land God had promised[3] was to be possessed by Israel. Having seen their affliction, God was going to deliver Israel to a very special place, a promised place of safety and comfort. The Book of Joshua records the details of how the Israelites must not just move into the region, but must also do battle with the current inhabitants. Trusting that the Lord was with them, Israelities moved into "their" land, after fighting for ownership. The people went as one, pledging their support and loyalty to Joshua. Spies were sent to Jericho to take stock of the enemy camp. The Jordan River was held back by miracle so the people could pass through. The Israelites followed Joshua and encountered the city of Jericho. Following the prescribed pattern, the Israelites surrounded the city, marching, shouting, trumpet blaring, and the walls of Jericho came tumbling down. Other than Rahab and her household, all the people and living things and devoted things were destroyed. This having been accomplished, the Israelites moved deeper into their Promised Land.

In a short time, they encountered another people and community. This one was much smaller and less well-protected than Jericho. It was a place called Ai. Only three thousand or so soldiers were sent from the Israelite camp to defeat Ai. The battle was indeed one-sided, but it was the warriors of Ai who defeated the Israelites. Upon hearing this news, Joshua cried out to God for a reason. God revealed to Joshua that their covenant had been broken. Someone from the Israelite camp had stolen some riches from Jericho against God's expressed wishes. The sin of Achan, a soldier overcome with greed, had caused much suffering for Israel. When his violation of the covenant was discovered, the Israelites destroyed his spoils of war and stoned him to death. Once the offering of repentance was made and the covenant renewed, God delivered a victory for the Israelite people at Ai. The conquests of the Israelite people spread among the other inhabitants of the land. The news that the God of the Israelite people traveled with them into battle was also spread among the communities. As word of the Israelites' travels spread, the settled populations were fearful. One group of people, the Gibeonites, lived about seven miles southwest of Ai. They were keenly aware of what had happened at Jericho and Ai. They were well informed that these Israelites had a covenant with God to possess their land.

The Gibeonites decided upon a clever ruse to deal with the Israelites. Instead of waiting to be defeated in battle, the Gibeonites went first to the Israelite camp. To have the Israelites believe they traveled from outside the Promised Land, they dressed in worn-out clothes, carried worn-out sacks, wore patched sandals, and carried food that was spoiled. Upon meeting the Israelites, they introduced themselves as people from far off who wanted to make a peaceful covenant. They sought protection from the Israelites, in return for which they would be their servants. Listen to the response of the people of Israel. "So the men partook of their provisions, and did not ask direction from the Lord. And Joshua made peace with them, and made a covenant with them, to let them live; and the leaders of the congregation swore to them."[4] Without asking questions or checking out the story from the Gibeonites, the Israelites made a covenant of peace with them. Without prayerfully seeking direction from the Lord, they offered lifelong protection to these unknown people. In their time, a promise was a promise. The Israelites had to honor their covenant. Even after they discovered the Gibeonites were really inhabitants of the land promised to them, the Israelites could not defeat them in battle.

In verse fourteen of this account is a very important phrase. This account was as true for the Israelites then as it is for us today. The text reads that the Israelites entered into a covenant with the Gibeonites, *and did not seek direction from the Lord.* When we honestly look at our lives today, as we begin to seriously seek spiritual direction, we need to ponder how seriously we have sought direction from the Lord. Do we prayerfully seek God's direction in our lives, or do we make covenants of our own accord? What kind of covenants do we make? With whom? With what? Many covenants that we have made are as unhealthy for us as the Gibeonite covenant was for the Israelites. Many covenants we have made violate our prior covenant with God. Our spiritual lives are tremendously affected by these covenants and we may not even recognize it. One of the first tasks we need to accomplish in removing our masks is to recognize our covenants. These particular covenants will, indeed, hinder our spiritual growth. Like the booty Achan had, we will need to do away with these and replace them with our true life-sustaining covenant with God. Some poorly made covenants that men make without first seeking direction from God may be the following:

- Real men should not express feelings.
- A man should not have spiritual longings for union with God.
- A man never feels, let alone admits, fear.
- If you fail at anything as a man, you are a failure.
- A man is only as important as his income.
- Spirituality is a woman's matter.
- A real man always has the answer.
- Men do not grieve wounds of rejection or abandonment.
- Sadness and hurt are not manly emotions.
- A man is put on earth to produce and perform.

All too many of us have made covenants with these and other beliefs which, in fact, are not under the direction of God. They come to us under clever ruse, they become familiar to us, and we live with them. From a deluge of public advertisements, scholarly traditions, family history, and oral tradition, men are encouraged to join these covenants. In fact, these covenants almost become commandments. In the following list, Solomon and Levy summarize these harmful covenants:

The Ten Commandments of Patriarchy

1. Thou shalt not cry or expose any feeling or emotion, fear, weakness, or empathy.
2. Thou shalt not be vulnerable, thou shalt be logical, rational, and thinking.
3. Thou shalt not listen except to find fault.
4. Thou shalt condescend to women in all ways, big and small.
5. Thou shalt control thy wife's body and relationships.
6. Thou shalt have no breadwinners before thee.
7. Thou shalt not be responsible for housework before anybody.

8. Thou shalt have no egos before thee.
9. Thou shalt have an answer to all problems and out-think every crisis.
10. Thou shalt never participate in any form in introspection.[5]

When a man keeps these covenants and obeys these commandments, when these are all that is familiar to him, he has no room for spiritual growth in Christ. A man who keeps these covenants and commandments has not first sought direction from God for his life, but will be a closely controlled, fearful, fragile individual. What will ring a bell for this man will be self-redemption and self-creation, two wholly impossible feats. The results of these covenants and commandments are quite evident:

- Men exist in incredible isolation and loneliness.
- Men have extremely difficult times forming trusting relationships.
- Men are driven to perform and produce all their lives.
- Men live outside their own bodies and souls, never being introspective.
- Men will view all other men as competitors.
- Because of unexpressed hurt and pain, men are chronically very angry.
- Compulsions and addictions are the result of men searching for love.
- Men's bodies frequently consume themselves out of despair.
- Men have fairly high levels of fear with commitment.
- To freely receive grace and mercy is unknown to men.
- A man is loathe to seek salvation from anyone but himself.
- Homophobia tends to hinder loving relationships with other men.
- Generally ignore or disparage the results of these covenants and commandments.
- The church has little or no support for men seeking spiritual growth.

When we fully appreciate the level at which these results will affect men, we begin to recognize the silent sufferings and pain of many men. Take this one step further. If many or most men exist

within these restrictive roles, the people with whom they relate—
lovers, family, friends, workmates, neighbors, churches, etc.—are
also affected by the unspoken brokenness of men. Not only will
men be hiding behind masks, but society will be shielded behind
them as well. So this book and these issues are really not just
"male" issues, but issues relevant to our entire society. The Gospel
of Mark introduced the Messianic secret. The Evangelist took great
pains to not reveal the person Jesus as the Messiah, the Son of God,
until the time was appropriate. This was to protect Jesus' ministry
so it would not be misunderstood as political in nature. Today, for
political correctness, we have a secret about men. We do not talk
about the pain, hurting, brokenness, and fears of men. This secret,
however, is not to protect a divine mission, it is to protect human
weakness. James Hollis brilliantly captures the essence of secrets
men carry. These secrets can be viewed as the ways men carry their
masks and deny themselves true identity. Here, Hollis directly con-
fronts conspiratorial covenants born of political correctness for men
to bear shame alone and silently.

The Eight Secrets Men Carry with Them

- Men's lives are as much governed by restrictive role expecta-
  tions as are the lives of women.
- Men's lives are essentially governed by fear.
- The power of the feminine is immense in the psychic economy
  of men.
- Men collude in a conspiracy of silence whose aim is to sup-
  press their emotional truth.
- Because men must leave Mother, and transcend the mother
  complex, wounding is necessary.
- Men's lives are violent because their souls have been violated.
- Every man carries a deep longing for his father and for his
  tribal fathers.
- If men are to heal, they must activate within what they did not
  receive from without.[6]

Our "Gibeonite problem" then, is our covenant with things that
come to us under deception and are not good for our souls. The eight
secrets men carry clearly illustrate the reality of these poorly made

covenants. At the same time, the results of the covenants are also exposed. In effect, we have not only made covenants with things such as loneliness, alcohol, excessive work habits, greed, envy, performance anxiety, shame, sexism, control, institutional religion, perfection, sexual compulsions, and fear, but we have also made a covenant not to talk about our covenants! Rare, indeed, is the man who will take off a mask or masks. This explains why, in part, it is difficult to begin or continue a community of men, or to have men gather to discuss masculine spirituality. This is a violation of the covenant before the covenants; that men just "should not talk about these things." The challenge to men who wish to reject this harmful tradition, and to the church helping these men, is thus twofold. First, give men permission and a place to no longer keep these secrets. Encourage men to openly discuss the pain of living behind outdated masks covering emotional and spiritual needs. Second, help men become experienced and comfortable with new covenants filled with new covenants full of communion with God given masculinity.

The church is openly invited to do what we do best, and what the Israelites forgot to do; turn first to God for direction. To help men become experienced in new covenants and to remove the old ones, we need God's direction. Let us turn to Scripture for an example.

In I Samuel 3:1-11, we read the account of the call of the prophet Samuel. Elkanah of Ramathaimzophim had two wives, Hannah and Peninnah. Hannah was barren, while Peninnah had children by Elkanah. After pouring her heart out to the Lord, and receiving counsel from Eli, the priest of the temple, Hannah was promised a son. In gratitude to the Lord she dedicated the child to holy service and gave Eli the boy to raise in the temple. Samuel was twelve years old, according to Jewish tradition, when he was delivered to the temple for dedication to the Lord. One evening Samuel was asleep within the temple of the Lord. The Lord cried out, "Samuel, Samuel!" and the boy Samuel went to Eli, believing he had called him. Eli told him he had not called him and sent the boy back to his chamber. This happened a second and a third time, until finally the priest Eli realized it was God calling the boy's name. Eli then instructed the boy to respond directly to the Lord if he again heard his name being called out. Indeed, upon the next calling Samuel responded, "Speak, Lord, for thy servant hears."

The way to a new covenant is found only through listening to the Lord call our names. God does call upon us by name, but we have been answering to family, friends, church, jobs, hobbies, secular psychologists, science, medicine, sports, etc. In fact, it is safe to say that most males today probably have no hope or inclination that God would directly speak to them. We just assume that any calling we have is from a human source. We even have thoroughly restricted God's calling to our clergy (who, astonishingly, must have their calling validated by secular counselors, psychological tests, and ecclesiological processes to make sure they are legitimate). It is as if God cannot speak directly to clergy or laypeople today without those persons being somehow suspect. It is part of the conspiracy of silence and the covenant of patriarchal individualism that God speaks no more. But this is not true. God continues to speak to us today. The real point is, that like Samuel, we do not listen well. This account from I Samuel reminds us that God can be heard, even today, when we listen and seek God's direction.

When I was in high school, my parents decided to take me on a vacation to France. We were to meet my older brother there and return home with him at the end of his foreign-exchange student program. This was a well-planned trip and was to include many stops at popular tourist sights around France. We were to fly to Paris, rent a car, and casually drive to Nice. This was a good plan. The problem, however, was that until we found my brother, no one in our traveling family spoke French. Getting the rental car itself was an amazing process that tested our patience (a quality not too available in our family). My father, a good American male, was loathe to ask for directions, particularly of a foreigner, so we had great difficulty getting around. Because we did not stop for help, along the drive from Paris to Nice we missed many of the things we had planned to stop and see. While at age fifteen I was amused to see hand gestures from the French that I had seen on the streets in Philadelphia, I was disappointed at our lost sightseeing opportunity.

When we do not ask for directions, we can miss a great deal. The American male seems particularly inclined to not ask for help or guidance. This is also true of men in our Christian faith. We have made some covenants of competition and performance and ego that will not allow us to appear lost or needy. We travel about at various speeds, in a multitude of directions, never stopping to ask for help from God. Just as Samuel, we turn to other sources, such as pride, greed, envy, gluttony, anger, laziness, and lust. However, when we do finally stop and seek the Lord's direction, we can be assured he will provide guidance. Along with James and John, Simon and Andrew, we can drop what we are doing and follow him. When we release ourselves from poorly and hastily made covenants, and join ourselves in faith to covenant with God, we will hear the Lord call our names and it will have a familiar ring of all truth and hope.

Chapter 2

Practical Use:
How to Use This Book

When I was about ten or eleven, somehow, I managed to survive the elimination rounds and I was selected to play baseball in a community league in Lansdowne, Pennsylvania. I did not really like or understand baseball. I did not follow the Phillies or any other baseball team for that matter, but most of my friends were on the team and I wanted to be with them. In any case, the so-called happy day came when I made the team. Even though this was an anxiety-producing time for me, I decided to make the best of it. When the coach asked me what position I wanted to play, I had to make a quick decision. Having surveyed the field a bit earlier, I noticed one player got to wear a lot of protective equipment. "Catcher," I told the coach, assuming I had just selected a very well-protected and safe position.

Very soon I had on my shin protectors, chest protector, batting helmet, groin protector flap, and face mask. That was great! I discovered two additional benefits afforded me by the face mask. First, no one could see my face or see into my eyes. They could not see the fear and anxiety on my face when I made a mistake. Nor could they see me close my eyes at some particularly scary moment. Second, I had a very limited view of the world outside my mask. I could see very little through the mask's metal bars. Consequently, I did not have to see the veins sticking out in my coach's neck or the frenzied parents in the bleachers. All my fears of inadequacy were well hidden by my face mask. I felt very safe and secure behind the mask. Being hidden was less painful than being revealed.

A mask is good for protection in baseball. The problem is, sometimes we forget to take off our masks when we leave the field. Not the metal external masks, but the internal masks, which are made of material with strength far greater than metal. We wear these masks because, sometimes in life, we need to emotionally, spiritually, and perhaps even physically, protect ourselves. When a baseball game is over, the catcher puts away his mask until the next game. In real life, many of us leave our masks on long after we need them. Eventually they come to feel like part of our face. The more masks we put on and keep on, the more limited our vision and our vulnerability. When we do not take our masks off, we are lost behind them from God, from others, and from ourselves. The masks that we have used to protect us from being hurt grow attached to us, and, before we know it, they hurt us. We live in isolation, fear, and numbness. At Jericho, Joshua and the Israelites learned that some walls had to come down. This was necessary for the growth of friendship, community, and love. We must take heed of this. We need to remember that our masks must come down if we are going to have any sense of full communion and union with the entirety of God's creation. This is particularly true for Christian men, who have, for generations, lived behind masks.

Interestingly, only recently have the needs of men been addressed in literature that speaks of spirituality. Most of this literature, however, has little connection to historic Christian spirituality. The need addressed in this book is Christian spiritual growth for men of the local congregation. This is informed by the ideas of contemporary writers of men's issues. We will use these ideas as building blocks upon the foundation already given to us by the church. We will help men redefine their spiritual beliefs, drawing together Scripture and experience. This will be spiritually beneficial to the men who participate, and help keep the church relevant in a rapidly changing society. This is an individual issue, and a societal issue.

> Men and masculinity in America are beginning to break down. This fact is of great concern to our whole society since most of our major cultural problems relate in some way to the collapse of masculinity; homelessness, crime, drug addiction, divorce, single-parent families, gang warfare, and so on. On an individual level, many men are also beginning to recognize the

masculine spiritual crisis in their lives in the form of father-wounds, alienation, emptiness in their work, collapsed relationships, and loneliness, to name a few. In the last few generations, these problems have grown too serious to deny or dismiss with a macho shrug of the shoulders. Men are beginning to face their challenges squarely.[1]

As men squarely face these challenges, the Christian community, through the local church, can be present to minister with them and support them in their times of spiritual change and transformation. This book provides direction for men of Christian churches to draw upon their history and tradition for spiritual growth. Men can seek out other men in a Christian community that challenges, sustains, and holds them securely in Christian faith and tradition. In so doing, they will not only benefit their own souls, but give praise to God. Jesus clearly calls us to be good companions, "A new commandment I give to you, that you love one another; even as I have loved you, that you also love one another. By this all people will know that you are my disciples, if you have love for one another."[2]

Our American culture is home to a plurality of theological and spiritual-direction concepts. The church must strive to appreciate the needs and struggles of a variety of people, and understand their issues of race, gender, ethnicity, and sexual orientation, etc. Christian traditions stand among other religious traditions trying to serve humanity in response to a loving compassionate God. These changes in today's society need to be addressed by the church. One of the changes is the need for an end to patriarchy, and the beginning of a good, healthy culture of masculine spirituality. On this issue Sam Keen writes:

> Deep down, the tectonic plates that have supported the modern world are shifting. Revolutions are daily occurrences; the centers of power are moving. Ancient enemies are making common cause. Paradigms and worldviews are changing overnight. Yesterday's certainties are today's superstitions. Today is all chaos and creativity. . . . The earthquake that is shaking men and women, their roles and their interrelationships, is part and parcel of this shifting of the world culture's tectonic plates. The changes in our gender roles are only one aspect of

the upheaval that accompanies the death on one epoch and the birth of another. And we will be in the birth process for several generations. For most of what feminists call Western history, men were considered the norm for humanity, the standard by which sanity and virtue were judged. Freud articulated the standard opinion when he asked with supposed seriousness, "what does a woman want?". . . . Feminist philosophers, theologians, and social activists have gone a long way toward articulating a systematic critique of modern society, re-defining female identity, and securing equal rights. They have made it abundantly clear that the answer to Freud's question is, and has always been, obvious to men of goodwill. First and foremost, women want what they have been denied—justice, equality, respect, and power. Today the question that is the yeast of the social dough is—"what do men want?"[3]

This book will help Christian men, who live amidst great social change, discover what they need and want through spiritual-growth activities. The church must sensitively listen to all people; women, African Americans, Asian Americans, the disabled, the poor, and the outcast. It must also address every person as an individual and not as a clone in a certain race or gender. As it does this, it honors God's creative spirit. The church must listen to the souls of men who are trying to end patriarchal domination, and orienting themselves as equals among equals. It will not be done quickly. It is work that now needs to begin as the role and relationships for men in society change.

This call for gender-specific communities is not new. Both the Roman Catholic and the Protestant communities have created communities and orders only for women and only for men. There is a serious need for the local church to create this type of gender-specific community for men where masculine spiritual growth can occur. In these communities, men can become more real, more vulnerable, more whole, and more alive. While it is too visceral to name, Keen seems to identify closely when he writes the following:

> we [men] need same-sex friends because these are the types of validation and acceptance that we receive only from our gendermates. There is much about our experience as men that can

only be shared with, and understood by, other men. There are stories we can tell only to those who have wrestled in the dark with the same demons and have been wounded by the same angels. Only men can understand the secret fears that go with the territory of masculinity.[4]

The need for gender-specific community is life-giving and unique. Hopefully, full acceptance of every man will be found in the community. On the original manuscript of his sermon entitled "You Are Accepted," theologian Paul Tillich penned in the margin these words, "for Myself."[5] That we are each accepted is the heart of Christ's message. It is the central mandate for Christ's church. One profound way for men to experience this grace of acceptance from God can be through participation in a masculine community for spiritual growth as set forth in this text. Tillich, a male theologian, shows us in this one brief and personal moment, how one man's soul reached out to God on a very intimate level. As a spiritual leader in the church, he illumines a path upon which other men can travel and the church can lead toward spiritual hope and blessing through acceptance. This note in the margin of a sermon shows us that some men do want a very loving and tender relationship with God through the church, and through personal experience.

Sadly, the type of desire for acceptance that Tillich expresses is consciously spoken by very few men; in fact, some men may not know that personal acceptance and relationship with God is possible. Acceptance is a bedrock issue for men. The church must help men identify this spiritual need, then help them meet it through acceptance from the Lord, and from one another. Patrick M. Arnold, an Old Testament scholar, captures the need for the church to offer this new form of ministry. He highlights personal acceptance and spiritual growth for men.

> Male estrangement from spirituality in Western Christianity is an old and complicated phenomenon finding its roots in an intricate web of historical factors ranging from psychology to sociology to economics. Men are responsible for this alienation from their native religiosity and it is they who must do the bulk of hard work in reconciling the split. Yet the church as an institution also bears responsibility for this great divorce,

for it has failed to understand men and to speak to them in a language they can comprehend. Except for isolated pastors and teachers, few Christian ministers seem to have a sympathetic notion of "what makes men tick," or empathy for their unique problems, or a clue how to solve those problems. If men are to help find the way to a vibrant Christian spirituality, they will need help from mentors who have already blazed their own trails and learned the delights as well as the hazards of the road. The church is worthless if it is unwilling or unable to help such people find their paths to God.[6]

The church, then, has a sincere and important call to minister with men. A large part of this ministry is of revelation. Revelation, the removing of masks, helps men be open to spiritual connection.

The masks that we wear present us with two particular spiritual problems. First, we cannot see God. Our spiritual vision is limited when we wear masks. Second, God cannot see us. If our souls and faces are covered with layers of masks, we are separated from God. We are in a place of spiritual wandering and isolation. Just as the Israelites in the desert, Elijah passing the brook at Cherith, Jonah fleeing from Nineveh, the two disciples on the road to Emmaus, and Saul on the road to Damascus, we wander without clearly seeing or clearly being seen. Consider your own life. What masks are you wearing? What hurts and vulnerabilities have you decided that no one would ever see again? What part of you are you protecting so strongly that even your own spouse, children, or God cannot see? Do you have friends—male friends—in whom you can confide with openness and trust? Can anyone confide in you? Do you have a commitment to God, or are you just going through the motions in your faith? Is Jesus Christ being fully revealed to you, or is your vision blocked? God took off all masks at creation. God wore no masks with the Israelites. God was seen quite plainly in the person of Jesus Christ. God wants to be seen, and God wants to see us. Of this truth there can be no doubt. Living without masks is obedient submission to a loving God. In our Western culture, where rugged individualism reigns as god, submission to God is a profound spiritual choice. The truth is, however, that self-redemption is a life behind a mask. It is a mask held in place by the myth of the tough guy.

If we look underneath the strong-man persona, much oppression becomes apparent in almost every area of a man's life . . . the deliberate "roughening up" of boys generally begins after birth, boys in America receive far fewer demonstrative acts of affection from their mothers than infant girls and are touched less. . . . Boys are also more likely to be held facing outward, toward the world and other people . . . boys are weaned earlier than girls, and receive an attitude of not needing or deserving as much love and nurturance as girls . . . boys are pushed out to be independent, aggressive and assertive. . . . Boys learn girls are allowed to have feelings, but peers, parents, and other adult authorities are uneasy if boys express feelings, as if feelings are not masculine. Men are taught to suffer alone and in silence . . . boys are often forced into showing no pain and to forego pleasure for pain to be a man . . . young boys are admitted to mental hospitals and juvenile institutions about seven times more frequently than girls of similar age . . . male infant mortality rate is higher than female, males are more prone to schizophrenia. All told, there are about two hundred genetic diseases that affect only boys . . . 90 percent of peptic ulcers are found in men, and men die of work-related injuries approximately twenty-to-one over women.[7]

Some men, Kipnis points out, are ready to end patriarchal control. These men seek new ways of living, and seek spiritual growth. He writes the following:

The Myth of the lone hero, who conquers all through the force of his will, is no longer the image that inspires the modern man in search of his soul. . . . Many men report that they feel alienated, alone, remote from the world, disconnected from their families and the community at large. They report that they have few—especially few male—friends and confidants. . . . Some men are numb. We're angry and confused about the double standards we encounter in many areas, the reverse sexism and rigid gender-role expectations. Many of us are isolated and uncertain how to break out of the old male stereotypes.[8]

To help Christian men make the transformation from outdated, stereotypical living, we do not expect instant results. It will take a very long time to turn the tide, but the determination and spiritual patience we use will not be in vain. A veteran at working with men, Owen-Towle states,

> Men usually ask, "What's in this for me? What are the benefits of a spiritually alive existence?" Americans are pragmatists and are skeptical about doing something without the prospect of positive results . . . spiritual discipline is an opportunity to stop thinking and talking compulsively and listen to the sounds of our interior homes.[9]

The miracle is, and the blessing of the Holy Spirit is, that, even against all odds, Christian men are asking for spiritual growth. Our church's theology and history has a wealth of information to deliver and a rock-solid foundation upon which these men can stand as they seek to remove their masks, and seek union with God.

> Jewish and Christian spiritual tradition contains powerful, challenging, and healing assets for men as they face the dangers, stresses and rapidity of modern life. Though modern liberal religion has lost awareness of male spiritual needs and even grown hostile to them, great resources for men still lie buried in the biblical and historical tradition. It is long past time to do a little consciousness-raising through a spiritual archeological expedition to find these treasures. The Bible is the focus . . . I write out of grief and pain. I hurt inside as I see the great divorce that has developed over the generations between men and Christian spirituality. I hurt for men that have lost the close contact with God that a healthy religiosity can nurture . . .[10]

We will endeavor to fuel this nurturing process with this text. I will identify in this book the eight masks that American Christian men typically wear. We hide behind these masks, and hope to protect ourselves or the image of ourselves. What is really happening is that our God-given desires are being covered up, and we are living a life far less than that which God created. There is a time to protect ourselves. People, events, and evil powers can indeed harm us. But there is also a time to take off the masks and be our true selves. Everything has a season. When we do take off our masks, this is as close to the beauty of the Garden as we can hope to reach. This is the central theme of our Christian faith, and of this book; seeing and being seen clearly by God in our created beauty. "Something like scales fell" from Paul's eyes and his faith was further revealed to him. This is a good imagery for how the removal of our masks may seem—suddenly life will come into focus. Let us now look at a list of the eight masks men wear and the companion list of the God-given desire they cover up.

THE MASK	*GOD-GIVEN DESIRE BENEATH*
Loneliness	Solitude and Community
Rage and Anger	Pain and Hurt
Compulsions	Love
Performance	Acceptance
Control	Friendship
Producing	Beingness
Competition	Humility
Institutional Religion	Spiritual Growth

Some, or all, of these masks are familiar to all Christian men in America today. If not, the word "denial" comes to mind, doesn't it? We frequently are lost as Christian men. Our lives show it. The life of the church shows it. Our society shows it. God did not create us to abandon our covenant. God sought after Abraham, Moses, Elijah, Jeremiah, James, John, Peter, and Paul. God seeks us today. We must experience this love, and the only way to do it, by the grace of God, is to live without masks covering our God-given desires for living the abundant life.

A mask did not put itself on, and it will not take itself off. With God's attending mercy, we must work to remove our masks. And, as nature abhors a vacuum and tries to fill it, we must be aware that once a mask is off something must fill its place. The recovering alcoholic may begin to smoke or the recovering sex addict may begin to overeat; one thing will seek to take the place of another. In the Christian faith, we have thirteen historic Christian disciplines that can help us remove our masks, and then help us fill the void the former mask leaves behind. For any man who is seeking to remove masks, keep them off, and discover the joy of Christian spirituality, these disciplines are invaluable. The disciplines are not "used" or "worked" in any certain order or at any certain time; they are ours to struggle with and celebrate over a lifetime. We do not one day "remove Mask A with Discipline 3." As we embrace the disciplines in our lives, over the years, the masks will slowly be identified naturally and just as naturally they will disappear. It is not magic; it is God's grace. None of this would begin, endure, nor end, without the grace of God.

The Holy Spirit of God, gifted to us on Pentecost Day,[11] will lead us in our discipline. We will be awakened, encouraged, convicted, forgiven, tested, befriended, loved, and seen by God through the Spirit. This is not a passive faith; we must also do our part. We must pray. We must repent. We must forgive. We must serve. And on through the disciplines we must travel. As Jesus encouraged Mary and Martha to each be content with their task, we must be content with the discipline given to us at any moment. This may not be easy, comfortable or familiar, but it is the Lord's way for us and we must accept it in faith. In a nation where people want immediate answers, definable results, and ironclad guarantees, Christian spiritual growth is almost foreign. Spirituality affirms the sovereignty of God and the spiritual world. The disciplines of our faith defy proof, immediacy, definition, and legal boundaries. The disciplines are, however, the real world to the Christian. The thirteen historic Christian disciplines we will focus on in this book are:

1. worship	8. fasting
2. prayer	9. surrender
3. service	10. confession/forgiveness
4. solitude	11. simplicity
5. financial commitment	12. friendship
6. body self-care	13. community
7. human sexuality	

Chapter 3 contains a thorough review of these disciplines that can help us remove our masks. We are each wearing masks that took years to construct and incredible energy to keep in place. They feel like part of our own skin now, and will not be very easily removed. Be prepared for some serious work, some absolutely joyous experiences of renewal, and a new season of revelation. A thorough reading of Scripture will reveal to you that each of these masks is found in the Bible, and that each of these disciplines is given to us by God. Do not expect to be perfect or quick at mask removal. Allow yourself to be patient, generous, and loving with your soul. Rely on the grace of God. Do not enter into a masculine style of works righteousness. Do not be discouraged if one discipline is more difficult for you than another. Try them all, and work with each over the years. Remember, too, that every mask you wear is there for a reason. You were hurt or scared and you protected yourself. The question is, do you still need the mask today? Yes, sometimes we are hurt today. Yes, sometimes we need masks of protection. But, just as the catcher in baseball, you have to know when to wear the mask and when to take it off. When we do not have a clear vision of God, or we are not seen plainly by God, when we do not have a clear vision of others and others cannot see us clearly, it is time for some mask removal.

Chapters 4 through 11 each deals with a mask, its attending issues, and end with questions to engage you in spiritual growth issues. These questions discuss the mask, your life, the Christian faith, and the thirteen disciplines. If you are participating in a group of men using this book, which is highly recommended, now is a good time to consider the issue of group leadership. The book is designed to be used by a man, individually, or during a nine-week program for men interested in Christian spiritual growth. Those working with this book alone will naturally set their own pace and method of proceeding. For those in a group setting, I suggest the group consist of about six to ten men, and that the meetings be held weekly in a private place. One man will need to offer leadership, but all members are responsible for the content and direction of the group. The first meeting should include primarily introduction type work. At the other eight meetings, I recommend the first hour or so be spent on discussing the book chapter and liturgy. Then, the second hour should be a time for men to openly reflect on how the issues from the reading and discussion affects him in his life. Everyone should have the book and read the book before the first meeting, and should then read the appropriate chapter during the week before the night for that topic discussion. It is hoped that every member can commit to being at every meeting. Without exception there needs to be a covenant of confidentiality. At the close of week nine, the group will want to discuss interest in continuing as a spiritual support group or other type of Christian men's group. Here are some things to keep in mind as the group forms and progresses.

GOOD LEADERSHIP

It is necessary for group leader(s) to have some experience in group work, men's work, and spirituality. Preferably all three, but at least one of these areas is necessary to ensure good leadership. The leader is also part of the group and should at all times conduct himself as an equal. I do not recommend bringing in any paid leaders. I think every congregation has at least a few men who could lead or even cofacilitate the meetings. Tilden Edwards identifies seven characteristics that the leader of a spirituality growth group needs. His suggestions are very good, and accurate. They are:

Leadership Characteristics

1. attentiveness to your own spiritual journey
2. trust in the Spirit's guidance
3. caring for the group
4. respect for the uniqueness and shared journey of each member
5. flexibility
6. awareness of basic group dynamics
7. basic knowledge of Christian aescetical tradition and human development[12]

The leader is well advised to provide leadership for what Edwards calls the "Primary Functions"[13] of a spiritual growth group:

- sanctuary—a safe environment
- teaching—introduction of concepts
- reflection—time to interpret and absorb

• accountability—for the self and the self-in-group
• time—keep good maintenance of schedule

Leadership is a challenge and a blessing, and a very integral part of the growth process. It may be desirable to have a different man lead the group each week.

EXTENSIVE ADVERTISING

Allow at least six months in advance for advertising to take effect. Not everyone reads church newsletters or bulletins regularly. Sometimes it is still helpful to offer multiple advertisement opportunities. Be sure to be clear in the purpose and the intent for the group. Men should be interested in spiritual growth, community, and being sincere. The class should not be filled under false pretense or guise of a "good old boys" meeting.

CHURCH-BASED LOCATION

Meet at the church on a regular basis, weekly for two hours at a time is best. Meet in private, where the group will not be disturbed. Light refreshments should be available and restrooms should be nearby. The men are encouraged to bring their Bibles, and have some available if necessary.

PREPARATION WITH TEXTBOOK

Books should be ordered well in advance and every man should have a book.

MEETING SCHEDULE

Meet for a minimum of nine weeks in succession. The first night should be a time to get acquainted and distribute books, review the liturgy and format, and introduce one another. Each succeeding night, one for each mask (Chapters 4-11), may best be used this way:

- *first hour:* Discuss one chapter each night, exploring how men relate to the content, (including any information from Chapters 1 to 3) and answer the questions at the end of each chapter.
- *second hour:* Use this time with no books or agenda. This is a free time for men to express their feelings, listen to one another, and share in the common issues of being a Christian man. This discussion may be limited to the topic of the night, or the topic may provide the door for proceeding to a significant related topic.

Most men will be relatively comfortable with the first hour. The second hour may be a new experience. This is where leadership is particularly important. A safe and caring atmosphere should be provided, where the men are free to open their souls to God and to one another. Issues and feelings that have been buried for years may surface. New insights into the faith may be spoken. This is the time to begin to lower masks and be sincere. The leader is cautioned to be aware of issues of denial, intellectualization, and avoidance. Above all, the second hour is a sacred and personal time, not a time for academic gymnastics or theological dogma. In these times, men are free to begin spiritual reflections, relating how their lives have been affected by Jesus Christ, where and how they hurt, or are joyous, and ways they struggle as Christian men. The tone of trust, acceptance, and confidentiality is essential here.

In the ninth session the men need to decide if they wish to continue meeting. It may be that some do, some don't, all do, or none do. Whatever the case, it is important to offer the option. The next weeks (or year's) agenda is then set by the group itself. The decision may be made to keep the existing format or switch to using the weekly meetings for all second-hour (interpersonal discussion) activities. The nine weeks would then have been used as a start into a very long journey the group will take together. For continuity and trust, I do not recommend letting anyone join the group after week four. I do not recommend that anyone leave the group without clearly stating why he is leaving.

BOUNDARY ISSUES

As may be seen in the "Code of Conduct," certain behaviors are allowed and certain others are not allowed. It is important that every man know this is a safe and nonthreatening environment. This code is not typically used in churches, but if the group is to form a solid trust and fellowship, written rules are essential.

NOT A CHURCH-REPORTING GROUP

This group is for spiritual growth. I recommend it fit loosely into the church organization, such as into the existing men's fellowship or under the sponsorship of the deacons. The group is not service-oriented, a voting body, political, a power block in the church, or a panel to undermine other groups. It is a unique, autonomous community of men seeking spiritual growth.

PATIENCE

Allow the Holy Spirit to work. This is a new venture with potential for great spiritual growth, but also some uncertainty. Any group I have participated in has been marked by awkward silence, seeming misdirection, power struggles, fear, anger, joy, love, pain, contentment, confusion, hope, anxiety, kindness, etc. Do not rush, and do not lose heart. The Spirit of God has much in store for each man and this group!

Please remember that this is not an academic textbook or a "how-to" manual; it is a workbook for masculine Christian spiritual growth. There is no exact right or wrong way to use the ideas in this book or limits to the potential way the spirit may move individuals or the group. Remember, too, that there is no such thing as a spiritual group "expert." If you are working in a group, the group needs to view its members as spiritual friends and equals. No university degree, career, income level, etc., makes one man more spiritual or spiritually correct than another.

Chapter 3

Thirteen Christian Spiritual Disciplines

My son, do not disregard lightly the discipline of the Lord, nor lose courage when you are punished by him. For the Lord disciplines him who he loves, and chastises every son whom he receives. "It is for discipline that you have to endure. God is treating you as sons; for what son is there whom his father does not discipline? If you are left without discipline, in which all have participated, then you are illegitimate children and not sons. Besides this, we have had earthly fathers to discipline us and we have respected them. Shall we not much more be subject to the Father of spirits and live? For they disciplined us for a short time at their pleasure, but he disciplines us for our good, that we may share in holiness. For the moment all discipline seems painful rather than pleasant; later it yields the peaceful fruit of righteousness to those who have been trained by it."

—Hebrews 12:5b-11

One of my new favorite passions is snow skiing. It is an absolute thrill to be on ski slopes and to ski down the mountains. It is truly just a delight to be within the entire ski area community. Since I am a novice, I receive my share of falling down experiences and getting lost on the trail. This is not too much fun, but it is part of the day. On one slope, I was able to ski down the entire mountain without falling, so I thought I was getting very good for a beginner. I went back up, got off the ski lift, and promptly fell flat on my face. I got up, skied for a while, and fell again. I went farther down the hill, turned, and made a wild spill. I finally reached the bottom of the

hill, sore, exhausted, and disappointed in myself. Waiting in line for
my lift chair, I just happened to reach down and check my ski boot
straps. Both straps on my right boot were loose. Somewhere along
the way, they had both slipped out of the clamp and hung loose, so
the boot was just loosely clinging to my foot and ankle. I tightened
both straps firmly. On my next trip off the lift and down the hill I
did not fall once. The lesson our instructor had taught us was certainly true, a loose ski boot will throw the skier. I made certain from
then on that I checked my boot straps every time I was on the lift.
Whenever I started to ski a hill, I knew my boots were properly
prepared.

For us to meet and navigate the course of life, we need to come to
the event properly prepared. To help prevent us from continually
falling, and to help us get back up and go well, we need to be ready
ourselves. Christian spiritual disciplines offer to us the strength of a
well-prepared soul which can sustain us in the twists and turns of
life. When we do the work, and it is a disciplined work, of participating in the thirteen Christian disciplines, we are ready to meet the
easy or complex challenges of life.

Having grown up in the 1960s and 1970s, I heard many messages
from within our culture such as: "Find the easy way," "Don't sweat
it," "The easier the better," and "Why work when you don't have
to?" In the advertising of the 1980s and 1990s, we have been
bombarded with messages of how to make things easier for ourselves and how to make computers, machines, appliances, or others
do our work for us. Work or effort seem to be equated with slow-
ness of mind or ineptitude. Throughout all four of these decades
there has been a constant theme in our society that quietly promotes
rejection of authority (not authoritarianism, just any type of authority), rebellion against authority figures (parents, teachers, pastors,
politicians, employers, God), and an abandonment of personal and
corporate discipline (remember the 1970s saying, "If it feels good,
do it")? These spoken and unspoken messages have not helped our
people be well prepared for the slopes of life. We are entering the
event of daily living without straps tight, or even without our boots
on at all. Lack of discipline, as we see with any child who lacks
good, loving, consistent discipline, results in confusion, choas, and
tremendous immaturity. When there is no spiritual discipline, there

is no spiritual direction or spiritual support. This results in a spirit that is flaccid, easily influenced by any source, inexperienced in matters of faith, and unable to meet the rigors and tests of life. To expect our souls to sustain us without any work of spiritual discipline is equivalent to trying to ski down an expert ski slope without tightened boots. It cannot be done.

To follow Jesus Christ as Lord and Messiah is to lose our own lives.[1] In a narcissistic culture such as ours, this is one tall order. To seek to listen to Christ first and culture a distant second (to forfeit the world and gain our lives), we need to be confident in our own identity and needs. We need to be fully prepared to meet the seductive advertising and political correctness of our times. To do these things, we need well-exercised souls, prepared for the competition of spirit versus world. This means we must lead lives of Christian discipline. We must first realize that discipline is good. Excessive discipline, or harsh punishment, is not good. But some experiences of this type of inappropriate treatment do not mean we should reject, in total, some discipline. The only way to exercise our souls and get some celebration of faith in them is to practice the disciplines of the Christian life.

In 1529 Gonzalo de Yepes and Catalina Alverez were united in marriage in Fontiveros, Spain. In 1542 their third son, Juan de Yepes, was born. Tragically, in 1545 Gonzalo died, and in 1547 the second child of their union, Luis, died. Dona Catalina, a woman of no means, went to her husband's wealthy family for assistance. She was flatly denied any help. Juan, whose father died when he was age two and whose brother died when Juan was age four, lived in poverty with his mother and one surviving older brother, Francisco. Moving to Medina del Campo, Juan was enrolled in a school for the poor. The place was run like an orphanage, with Christian doctrine as its foundation. Showing an interest in the sick and needy, and being an excellent scholar, Juan was enrolled in a Jesuit school at age seventeen. At age twenty-one, he left the Jesuit tradition for the Carmelite order. It seems that Juan, now named Fray John of Matthias, was drawn to the Carmelites because of the emphasis upon the contemplative spirit. In 1567 he was ordained a priest and began to celebrate mass. At his first post in Medina, John met Madre Teresa de Jesús (Theresa of Avila), a Carmelite leader for the community of nuns. Their relationship was powerful for both them and their orders. Together they sought to deepen their spiritual lives and to influence the training of Carmelite clergy and nuns toward the contemplative direction. John's work and influence began to grow, as did his commitment to the Carmelite tradition. Changing his name to John of the Cross, he fully embraced the contemplative aspect of spiritual growth. John of the Cross never forget his calling or his own life experiences and dedicated much of his life to teaching the city's poor and homeless children to read and write.

A conflict of interest in jurisdiction and religious order began to evolve for John of the Cross and the Carmelites in 1575. King Philip II felt religious-order reform was part of his duty. During his reign, the church made several decisions regarding administrative matters and accountability in Piacenza, Italy, without consulting him. Miscommunications occurred, the king was angry because he felt left out of the decision process. John of the Cross became caught in this ever-tangling web of political and religious confusion when he tried to follow decisions of his Carmelite order, even though they were in contradiction to decisions made at Piacenza. With no friendly papal nuncio to defend him, he was found in violation of the King's orders. On December 2, 1577, Carmelite laypeople broke into John of the Cross's quarters at Avila, Spain, and seized him by force. With the approval of his order's visitator, or leader, he was blindfolded, handcuffed, and taken to a monastary in Castile. There, John of the Cross, imprisoned over a political/ religious jurisdictions battle, was asked to recant his work. He would not, but instead confessed his calling to be legitimate and properly ordained by the church. For over two months he was locked in the prison of the monastery.

> His accusers locked him first in the monastery prison, but at the end of two months, for fear of an escape, they moved him to another spot, a room narrow and dark, without air or light except whatever filtered through a small slit high up the wall. The room was six feet wide and ten feet long. There John remained alone, without anything but his breviary, through the terribly cold winter months and the suffocating heat of summer. Added to all this were the floggings, fasting on bread and

water, wearing the same bedraggled clothes month after month without being washed—and the lice.[2]

Imagine, just for following orders, a man under command, he was treated so dangerously and brutally by men of his own Order. The suffering and pain he had to endure, for his faith and commitment to Jesus Christ and the discalced Carmelite Order, was outrageous. It was not until August, some nine months into his captivity, when he was allegedly quite close to death, that John of the Cross made his escape. One can only imagine how difficult this would have been for a beaten, starved, isolated, and betrayed contemplative priest.

> John chose life and undertook a dangerous escape plotted during the short periods out of his cell. . . . When the friars seemed asleep and the house all still, he pushed hard on the door of his prison and the (already loosened) lock came loose. . . . By means of a kind of rope made out of strips torn from two old bed covers and attatched to a lamp hook, he escaped through the window onto the top of the wall.[3]

While in the Toledo prison in 1578, John, later known as St. John of the Cross, wrote many poems, including "The Spiritual Canticle," containing thirty-one stanzas. Immediately after this time, or perhaps sometime while in prison, he wrote the poem "The Dark Night," followed by a Commentary on the same writing in 1584. During this same time, he wrote the treatise, "The Ascent of Mount Carmel." In these latter two texts, as in all the writings of St. John of the Cross, are the themes of: union with God, the Trinity and its offices, the mystery of union with Christ, active and passive faith development, and the constant pressure of human sin upon the soul. The Bible was the sole source for his writings, which include very personal accounts of his own spiritual struggles and words for fellow pilgrims. These words from St. John of the Cross are very intimate and revealing of his own inner life and the human need for unity with God as Creator, Redeemer, and Sustainer. His mark on Christian spirituality can never be underestimated or forgotten.

For the purposes of this book and this chapter on the Christian spiritual disciplines, I want to highlight two important components from these inspiring writings of St. John of the Cross; the passive and active nature of spirituality. To do this properly, we must first consider the man to whom we now attend. Padre Fray John of the Cross, Discalced Carmelite, was a man of very humble beginnings. Fatherless, poor, turned out by his family, living in a poverty stricken village, and with little hope, he was given to the public schools to be raised when his mother found herself unable to support him. As a scholar in his field of theology he excelled, and was found to be quite compassionate with the elderly and infirm. He had a natural sense of calling to a life of contemplation and to ministry as a vocation. With a series of choices to make in the church, he made none routinely or without considerable prayer. He unwittingly became involved in a political dispute that led to imprisonment at the hands of his own church people. Suffering immensely, grossly mistreated and deprived of light, good food, companionship, liquids, and freedom, in desperation he escaped imprisonment, hid for a while, and began to write about the spiritual aspects of his journey. All the while, he was fervently involved in his own contemplative life and a life of outward good works in the community. Constantly, and consistently, St. John of the Cross sought union with God. His life was an open book on the value of keeping Christian discipline. As the writer of Hebrews taught, his discipline led to a life of holiness.

This being said, I want to visit a common thread that gently and obviously weaves its way through "The Ascent of Mount Carmel" and "The Dark Night." When followed, the common thread in these two writings provides considerable guidance for us in our work of Christian spirituality. When we seek the ultimate goal of Christian discipleship, union with God, the common thread between the two writings, supported by the grace of God, will serve us well.

The common thread that runs throughout both writings is that spiritual discipline is both active and passive, and includes both the sensual and the spiritual. First, we will discuss the active pursuit of union between God and human. St. John of the Cross believed that one had to actively pursue an intimacy with God. Through contemplative prayer, benevolent actions, Bible reading, communion within a community, and the Sacraments and Rites of the church, one was required to actively pursue this relationship. In the pure pursuit of these disciplines, one must do two things: first, still the sensory part of the soul; and second, still the human spiritual appetites. Let us look to the first two verses of "The Ascent of Mount Carmel" for example.

> One dark night,
> fired with love's urgent longings
> —ah, the sheer grace!—
> I went out unseen,
> my house being now all stilled.
> In darkness and secure,
> by the secret ladder, disguised,
> —ah, the sheer grace!—
> in darkness and concealment,
> my house being now all stilled.

The "night" for him is a representation of the deprival of gratification of the flesh. This is the active denial of one's narcissistic drives. In the prison at Toledo he experienced the total denial of his own desires. He was unable to move about freely, or care for his bodily functions properly; he was beaten, isolated, and under the constant watch of another. In this loss of control, he learned to surrender his own sensual desires. In poetry he records this event, "my house being now all stilled." The "dark night of the soul," (a term used so flippantly today among self-help writers) was born here, but it was no easy birth. The dark night is a time of pain, fear, isolation, uncertainty, and surrender. It is a time to actively release the soul from all sinful and worldly desires. In his exposition of the first stanza, St. John of the Cross reminds the reader of David's writings about this "torture": "The cords of my sin, my appetites, have tightened around me."[4] David is very graphic about the enslavement and torture one's own sensual desires can inflict. "They circled around me like bees, stung me, and burned me like fire among thorns."[5]

The first discipline, then, is to actively quiet these "bees," the sensual appetites of the flesh. For St. John of the Cross these appetites do not come from outside the self—they live in the soul. It is, then, in essence, that the soul must quiet itself from distractions within.

The second night, referred to in the second stanza, is the activity of our spirit. Awakened from within, once the soul is quiet, where it has been concealed, the spirit actively stretches a path, or ladder, toward God. The biblical imagery of Jacob is certainly alive here. Again led by grace, one now actively seeks the second step, active spiritual surrender. The soul, which lives in darkness, now actively goes beyond itself and builds a connection toward union with God. "But all that is required for complete pacification of the spiritual house is the negation through pure faith of all the spiritual faculties and gratifications and appetites. This achieved, the soul will be joined with the Beloved in a union of simplicity and purity and love and likeness."[6] The active cleansing of the spirit to St. John of the Cross is much more frightening, and a darker journey, than the first night, the cleansing of the flesh. He even refers to the active sensory cleansing as "twilight" and this second active cleansing of the spirit as "midnight." It must begin in utter darkness, and it is also a journey of faith, which is from darkness. This part of the dark night is not too well understood today, because most authors stop at the first night. In our society's movement for quick fixes and expediency, we miss the subtle, but dramatic, movement of this second stanza. For the Christian, the journey is only half made if we skip the second stanza, the negation of our selfish spiritual desires. The purity, and the utter essence of union with God in this writing, is utterly magnificent and beyond the knowledge of any theological construct or dogma of the church. This is spiritual peace, a "resting in union" with God. Perhaps remembering his own fragile journey or through his attatchment to teaching the masses, St. John of the Cross wrote a very simple illustration to talk about this profound imagery:

A ray of sunlight shining on a smudgy window is unable to illumine that window completely and transform it into its own light. It could do this if the window were cleaned and polished. The less the film and stain are wiped away, the less the window will be illumined; and the cleaner the window is, the brighter will be its illumination. The extent of illumination is not dependent on the ray of sunlight but on the window. If the window is totally clean and pure, the sunlight will so transform and illumine it that to all appearances the window will be identical with the ray of sunlight and shine just as the sun's ray. Although obviously the nature of the window is distinct from that of the sun's ray (even if the two seem identical), we can assert that the window is the ray or light of the the sun by participation. The soul on which the divine light of God's being is ever shining, or better, in which it is ever dwelling by nature, is like this window, as we have affirmed. A soul makes room for Gód by wiping away all the smudges and smears of creatures, by uniting its will perfectly to God's; for to love is to labor to divest and deprive oneself for God all that is not God. When this is done the soul will be illumined by and transformed in God. . . . Consequently, we understand with greater clarity that the preparation for this union, as we said, is not an understanding by the soul, nor the taste, feeling, or imagining of God or of any other object, but purity and love, the stripping off and perfect renunciation of all such experiences for God alone.[7]

This is no easy task. He is aware of how guilt, sin, desires of the flesh, and worldly concerns can torture a soul. Few are the faithful who can make the ascent beyond here.

The second part of this common thread is the passive night. In prison, St. John of the Cross discovered he could "do" nothing. After all his freedom was taken away, he was left alone in the dark. After he actively cleansed his sensory and spiritual appetites, he experienced a whole new dark night. In this night he was able to only be passive. He was unable to "do" anything for himself, of flesh or spirit. This was the time to be passive, and receive God's gifts. He quotes the great prophet Isaiah to tell us how difficult the active purgation is, but how it is also necessary to lead to this passive blessing: "In your presence, O Lord, we have conceived and been in the pains of labor and have brought forth the spirit of salvation."[8]

In this passive night, we are beyond our own ability, beyond our own appetites, and only open to receive the light of salvation God has to offer. Freed from the house of our own senses to live in the house of God's love. This is a time when we are in complete union with God. Because we have had to set aside and still our own sensual and spiritual desires, and let our entire being be submitted to the mercy of Christ, one can appreciate the transformation that will occur. As St. John of the Cross elucidates, this is a frightening and torturous process, but one that leads to unfathomable goodness and grace. It is the fruitful activity of removing the masks that cover our true spiritual communion with God. The gifts of the Holy Spirit— love, peace, joy, kindness, gentleness, patience, faithfulness, goodness, and self-control—will no longer be abstract ideas, but spiritual realities in our flesh and soul.

For the purposes of this book and our ever-evolving spiritual growth, we are reminded of the common thread in these writings. We are also reminded that all of this takes place by the grace of God, nothing is earned or cleverly devised by the human mind in this night. With these things in mind, let us now look at the thirteen classic spiritual disciplines of the Christian faith. These are the active spiritual efforts we can make, with the blessing of the Holy Spirit, to cleanse our sensual and spiritual appetites. These are also the disciplines for the passive night, and the truest sense of union with God. As St. John of the Cross has told us, and Abraham, Moses, Elijah, Job, James, John, Paul, Peter and Jesus himself have shown us, spiritual discipleship takes work. It is difficult, fearful, and sometimes confusing and painful, but it is necessary for spiritual growth. The union of God waits within and beyond these disciplines. We need be passively and actively exercising our souls with them for the journey. Please, again remember, this is not a works-righteousness motif, it is the Spirit which guides us along this path. As Jesus was led by the Spirit in the wilderness of his temptations, where he was both active and passive to prepare for his ministry, we are being prepared, and led.

Thirteen Christian Spiritual Disciplines

1. worship
2. prayer
3. service
4. solitude
5. financial commitment
6. body self-care
7. human sexuality
8. fasting
9. surrender
10. confession/forgiveness
11. simplicity
12. friendship
13. community

Union with God is the goal of Christian spirituality. Active and passive spiritual discipline is a means to the goal. The Holy Spirit is the vessel which directs, encourages, and invites us along this powerful and sacred journey. Along the way, we must purge ourselves of our appetites of the flesh and the spirit. These disciplines are the classic ways a Christian removes the masks of selfish appetite and reveals oneself to God. We will be drawn into the dark night of our souls, in its most humbling and terrifying aspects. Beyond this is the union of which words ineffectively speak. Like the Israelites after the Exile and Christians after their persecution, we must do the *work* of building our faith. Trusting in God, we actively engage in these disciplines. Then, or even simultaneously, trust in God and we passively engage in these disciplines. In this manner, we prepare our souls for the blessings of purgation and union. Remember, as was written to the Hebrews: ". . . for the moment all discipline seems painful rather than pleasant; later it yields the peaceful fruit of righteousness to those who have been trained by it."[9]

WORSHIP

Our worship of God grows naturally out of the soul's desire to be in union with God. Not only does God command our worship, "You shall have no other gods before me,"[10] but Jesus tell us as well, "You shall worship the Lord God and him only shall you serve."[11] To worship God is to discover and rediscover God, as the central focus of our lives and all our spiritual growth exercises. "The 'remembering' of God, of which we sing in the Psalms, is simply rediscovery, in deep compunction of the heart, that God remembers us. In a sense, God cannot be remembered. He can only be discovered."[12] To worship God is to focus our entire being on God, so that in all we do we are bringing ourselves into closer and more intimate relationship. In Paul's letter to the church at Rome,[13] and in the writings of St. John of the Cross, we are reminded that both God, and the potential for sin, exist within us. Worship is a way to purify ourselves and cleanse ourselves of this inner sin, opening our souls to discover God who already exists there. Worship, then, is both a joyous and a fearful time, for it will mean the surrender of our sensual and spiritual selfishness and submission to the mercy of Christ.

"Worship" is not limited to one hour of formal activity on a given day of the week. Worship of God can be celebrated in the mutuality of a good friendship, recycling glass and aluminum, visiting the sick and needy, abstaining from alcohol and drug, mentoring children, and everyday activities of faithfulness. To begin the process of removing our masks is a form of Christian worship. We as Christians in America have been to quick to limit and compartmentalize our faith. Worship is not "done," it is celebrated every moment we draw breath. This affirms, like the old Hebrew belief, that all of life is a sacred gift from God. Just as sexual foreplay may occur during a meal or an evening at the beach or in simple conversation, building a heightened awareness and anticipation of the other, worship prepares us slowly for intimacy with God. The former is consumated with sexual union and communion, the latter with spiritual union and communion.

PRAYER

This discipline has been given to us by Jesus himself, who both preached and practiced prayer. Jesus teaches us how to pray,[14] showed us his own prayers,[15] and even prayed for us.[16] Seeking more faithfulness, the disciples once even asked Jesus how to practice this discipline.[17] Prayer, as a discipline, defies definition. Prayer need come from the soul, and be unfettered by pride, hypocrisy, or selfishness. Prayer can be of a confessional nature. Prayer can be of petition seeking God's help, for oneself or another. Prayer can be of a supplicatory nature, asking God to intervene in events of human life. Prayer can be of a contemplative nature, asking God to open and enter one's soul. Prayers can be uttered in public or private, and can include any thought, feeling, or need of the human heart, mind, and soul.

In his first letter to the church at Thessalonica, Paul urged the people, among other things, to "pray constantly."[18] This admonition is clearly valid for us today. From the Jesus prayer; "Lord Jesus Christ have mercy on me, a sinner," to a day or weekend set aside for prayerful communication to God, this discipline is readily available to all the faithful. Father Henri Nouwen recommends that three criteria need be met for praying: "a contemplative reading of the word of God, a silent listening to the voice of God, and a trusting obedience to a spiritual guide."[19] Prayer is not a willy-nilly exercise, or one to be done once and then tested for immediate results. Prayer is one part of a disciplined life.

SERVICE

Christian service is a discipline which calls for us to place our faith in action. It is recorded that Desert Father Silvanus once said: "Woe to the person whose reputation is greater than his work."[20] Here he gives us an appreciation for the fact that service is an integral part of one's responsibility to God on the path to spiritual growth. Service as allowing oneself to serve, and service as in the form of physical labor, are part of this discipline. Jesus, the servant of God and servant of the people, was the best example we have of this discipline. Recall Jesus' words: "whoever would be great among you must be your servant. . . even as the Son of Man came not to be served but to serve."[21] There is indeed no faith without good works. Service as a Christian discipline can take on a variety of faces: teaching, serving the homeless, studying, Habitat for Humanity, care of church property, Meals on Wheels, scouting leadership, positions in the local congregation or the denomination, etc. When we serve, we are saying that God is greater than we are, that we are a part of creation, that our gifts are to be shared, and that other people are of value. This discipline calls for a lifetime of participation in the building of the Kingdom of God.

SOLITUDE

Solitude is a particularly important discipline to begin at the start of one's spiritual journey. We need to awaken our souls to all the patterns and uniqueness of our own personality, and this can only be done in solitude. Here, alone, we rekindle a sense of love and acceptance of ourselves. Not ourselves in isolation, but ourselves in union with God, apart from the rest of humanity. To be alone, and feel lonely, or to constantly fear being alone, is a significant hint that our souls are not at peace. Surely in a society that constantly advertises ways to occupy our time and effort, one must be very disciplined about finding and developing solitude. Particularly for men, who are encouraged to perform and produce, solitude is both a feared, and much needed, discipline. "Sometimes one wonders if the fact that so many people ask support, advice, and counsel from so many other people is not, in large part, due to their having lost contact with their innermost self."[22] Solitude is spending time with one's self. Solitude as a discipline is creating that time and listening to one's soul. With the presence of God in our souls, we are never alone. So, in solitude, we chance a wonderful opportunity to hear God. Jesus was known to frequent a style of solitude when his life was particularly difficult.[23] Sometimes in Jesus' solitude he was literally alone; other times he was in community. Solitude, then, is not as much a physical matter as it is an internal, spiritual discipline. How can we be part of the community, but also maintain our own individual identity? Peter, for instance, when he denied Jesus three times, betrayed Jesus and his own sense of solitude. He allowed his soul to become occupied by fear and laziness. Solitude as a discipline places the world outside our soul and Jesus within it. St. John of the Cross, as described in Chapter 2, is a very good example of the struggle, and the fruits, of this particular discipline.

FINANCIAL COMMITMENT

"Where your treasure is, there also shall be your heart."[24] Money, and what we do with it, speaks richly about our spirituality. Our nation spends most of its dollars on national defense, and least of its dollars on education and childcare. What does this say about us? Perhaps that we want to protect what we have more than we want to mentor and care for our children. This may sound a bit harsh, but the subject of money is rather clear-cut as a Christian spiritual discipline. Our nation is becoming filled with two classes rather than class equality, and we are witnessing a significant decrease in financial contributions to churches and secular benevolent organizations. In America, money is status, pride, worth, power, and control. One is loathe to do without, or give it up.

For the Christian, we must consider money a spiritual discipline. How, or how little, do we commit our personal finances to Christ's body on earth?

> . . . And he said to them, "Take heed, and beware of all covetousness; for a man's life does not consist in the abundance of his possessions." And he told them a parable, saying, "The land of a rich man brought forth plentifully; and he thought to himself, What shall I do, for I have nowhere to store my crops?" And he said, "I will do this: I will pull down my barns, and build larger ones; and there I will store all my grain and my goods. And I will say to my soul, Soul, you have ample goods laid up for many years; eat, drink and be merry." But God said to him, "Fool! This night your soul is required of you; and the things you have prepared, whose will they be?" So is he who lays up treasure for himself, and is not rich toward God."[25]

Financial commitment is a spiritual discipline.

The invitation to us is to not just share a portion of what we have received, but to discipline our lives around Jesus Christ. The more we store up, financially and spiritually, the more we destroy our own spritual growth and the Kingdom of God. This calls for a radical reordering of our priorities, and more often than not a radical reordering of the priorities of our churches. The Christian and the church that is wealthy in savings and endowments will want to seriously consider their stewardship of this spiritual discipline of financial commitment. The above parable from Luke cannot be misinterpreted.

BODY SELF-CARE

Your body is the temple of the Lord.[26] This is the best reason I know of for understanding body self-care as a Christian spiritual discipline. St. Paul is very clear on the spiritual nature of the body when he writes, "So glorify God in your body."[27] This flesh, bone, sinew, muscle, tissue, and blood that sustains our humanity as a vessel of the Lord needs our love and attention. God breathed life into our lungs, and God created us in his own image. We are a very holy creation and we need to be good stewards of our bodies. This is clearly a form of worship of God.

After my surgical experience, and long period of recovery, I had to familiarize myself with my body all over again. Certain parts no longer worked as they had before, and certain areas had no feeling because nerves were cut. I discovered how much I had taken my body for granted before this trauma. I also learned that to enjoy service, solitude, worship, and the other disciplines; I had to be comfortable in my own body. Fatty foods, excessive sugar, alcohol, drugs, tobacco, caffeine, too little or too much exercise, and too little sleep take their toll on our bodies, and on our souls. When Jesus cautioned the disciples to carry little with them and to not worry about the mundane, this was a good call for us to care for our bodies. Not the external looks, but the internal being. James Nelson writes:

> For most of the Christian era we have mistrusted, feared, and discounted our bodies. That remains strangely true in modern cultures such as ours, which frequently glorify and even idolize the body (or at least certain idealized expressions of it). One result of this mistrust is that we have not taken our body experiences very seriously in doing our theological reflecting.[28]

He writes that we experience and know God through our bodies. To care for our bodies, with proper diet, rest, exercise, and annual physicals is to love ourselves, love God, and be disciplined in our relationship with God.

HUMAN SEXUALITY

The history of the Christian tradition has been fairly consistent with regard to human sexuality—we choose to ignore it or shame it. When the early church subscribed to a dualistic approach to being human (the spirit is good and superior and the body is not good and inferior) the pattern was set and remains today. Spirituality was conducted from outside the body or separate of the body, where holiness was equated with sexlessness and bodilyness.

> After the Reformation of the sixteenth century, differences in Roman Catholic and Protestant spirituality began to emerge. The Catholic tradition had accented the individual's own effort toward union with God, union involving both purgation and illumination. The Protestant mode now emphasized the joyful experience of gracious forgiveness, leading to sanctification. The sanctity or holiness toward which one was enabled to grow was not so much a process of following deliberate rules and special spiritual practices under the supervision of a spiritual director, but now more the devotional and moral disciplines that one accepted for the living of all life. While the differences between Catholic and Protestant spiritualities can be unfairly exaggerated, they were there. But two things remained common to both. One was that proper spirituality and the means thereto were generally defined by the male church leadership. The second, not suprisingly, was that spiritual holiness was largely disconnected from body and flesh. Indeed, the idea that Christian spirituality might involve the celebration of one's flesh, the affirmation and healing of one's sexuality, and an earthy, sensuous passion toward life was largely foreign.[29]

The discipline we need to exercise today for spiritual growth is acceptance and healthy celebration of our sexuality. We must first acknowledge as a church that we have inappropriately separated body from flesh, and spirituality from sexuality. Now we must do the work of reuniting them. Union with another, of flesh and spirit, is the height of human relationship. This may occur during actual intercourse, or during conversation, at play, or in united prayer. The stereotype of sex as "an act" is dismal compared to the beauty of sexuality as an expression of acceptance, communion, and trust—a spiritual blessing. Spirituality is the effort to unite with God. Human

---

Extracted material has been quoted from *Body Theology* by James Lilson © 1992. Westminster/John Knox Press. Used by permission.

sexuality is the effort to unite with another human. Both of these efforts are God-given and both of them contain fleshy and spiritual discipline. Both of them are also born of the same desire—love.[30]

FASTING

This discipline may be the least popular and most misunderstood avenue of spiritual growth. Nonetheless, fasting is clearly a Christian spiritual discipline. Both Hebrew and Christian tradition speak of the need for fasting in developing one's spirituality.[31] These biblical accounts tell us that fasting was for spiritual purposes, not for vanity or social acceptance. The prophet Joel indicates that fasting was even a mandatory part of response to a national emergency: "Blow the trumpet in Zion, sanctify a fast, call a solemn assembly, gather the people."[32]

Fasting in the church calendar grew popular for atonement or as an obligatory rite over the years, beginning with Moses' first call to fast.[33] The Pharisees observed a strict fasting discipline twice a week, usually Monday and Thursday.[34] It is reported that John Wesley "felt so strongly about this matter, that he refused to ordain anyone to Methodist ministry who did not fast on two days."[35] Jesus was very clear that fasting was an important discipline to him.[36] Fasting is a way to increase awareness of our bodies, give honor to our Creator, cleanse the system, and find peace and contentment with less. This discipline, with sound spiritual advice, can be kept by us today with little effort. The bond between body, soul, earth, and the Divine is nourished when we engage in the discipline of fasting.

SURRENDER

This is probably the most difficult spiritual discipline, for man or woman. Jesus said, "If any man would come after me, let him deny himself and take up his cross and follow me."[37] Here, he calls Christians to a sense of commitment, self-denial, submission, and spiritual direction. The opposite of this is our innate drive toward self-satisfaction and things of narcissistic pleasure. The surrender of which Jesus preached, taught, and lived was not self-deprecating or abusive, but faithful and trusting. It is the emptying of one's own agenda and replacing the emptiness with the agenda of God. Since we spend our whole life trying to be self-sufficient, surrender of our will and control is a terrorizing concept. But, nonetheless, this is Christ's calls to us. St. Francis of Assisi, St. John of the Cross, Mary the Mother of Jesus, Jonah, Paul, Joseph, Moses, and so many others are examples of surrender to God. This is a soul-level commitment that we are not in control, but are obedient children of God.

The discipline of surrender is not to be confused with powerlessness, victimization, or self-hatred. For in this movement, we are not wiping out the self but joining the self with God. This is undoubtedly why Jesus said, "He who finds his life will lose it, and he who loses his life for my sake will find it."[38] In my own hospital experience, I did not consciously seek this surrender; it was thrust upon me. Yet, even now, I am deeply moved by the experience, and am forever marked with the spiritual blessing of surrender. God's grace is most certainly active in seasons of surrender, for how else could we withstand the magnitude of the moment?

In his *Spiritual Exercises*, St. Ignatius of Loyola writes, "Human persons are created to praise, reverence, and serve God the Lord and by this means to attain salvation. The other things on the face of the earth are created for us, to help us in attaining the purpose for which we are created."[39] Surrender is an act of full participation in God's creation, and therefore a celebrative act of salvation for humankind. Surrender is an act of love for God, a discipline that will help us draw closer to our Creator, and away from solely earthly desires. So, when Paul writes that "He . . . emptied himself, taking the form of a servant,"[40] we understand the totality of surrender, letting go of those things which will keep us from more fully serving God.

CONFESSION AND FORGIVENESS

Confession offers us the opportunity to cleanse our minds and souls of sinful actions, thoughts, memories, or feelings, and to receive forgiveness. We are cleansed and we start anew. Jesus Christ, Holy Mediator,[41] earned this grace for us on the cross at Calvary. As believers, men are entrusted to hear the confessions of one another, and to offer, in the name of Jesus Christ, the forgiveness of God. Jesus declares this to be true when he says, "If you forgive the sins of any, they are forgiven; if you retain the sins of any, they are retained."[42] To confess is to name, in writing, orally or prayerfully, the specific thing or things we have done in violation of God's word. In so doing, we cleanse our soul and mind of the sin, and seek forgiveness. We do this not for its own sake, but to receive the mercy of God, "If we confess our sins, God is faithful and just to forgive us our sins, and cleanse us from all unrighteousness."[43] Our confessions, in detail, will draw us closer to God, to our own sense of wholeness, and to others. In confession we admit our sin, and at the same time we praise God whom we trust to forgive us. Confession is an act of trust, and a deep desire for love. Confession, when carried out with a trusting person, can provide a watershed of grace and hope, through the mercy of God. The more we do confess and remove the shame and despair of sin from our souls, the more room we have for other disciplines.

SIMPLICITY

I pass two malls, three major shopping centers, and a myriad of little stores on my way to and from church everyday. These stores, by and large, sell the same things. Inside them, the stores almost look alike and are set up the same way. We process, sell, and traffic in so much "stuff" that the excesses in our culture are astounding. We bombard ourselves with things we believe we must have, or things that show others we have them.

Jesus told the disciples, and tells us, that simplicity is the true discipline to help control our excesses and keep us focused on the Kingdom of God. Recall that when the Twelve Apostles were commissioned, Jesus said; "Take nothing for your journey, no staff, nor bag, nor bread, nor money; and do not have two tunics. And whatever house you enter, stay there, and from there depart."[44] He sent the Seventy out with a similiar mission call to simplicity; "Go your way; behold, I send you out as lambs in the midst of wolves. Carry no purse, no bag, no sandals; and salute no one on the road."[45] Simplicity is commitment to Christ. To be able to offer ourselves to God's kingdom, we cannot be cluttered with all sorts of earthly trappings. Paul wrote, ". . . for whether we live we live unto the Lord, and whether we die we die unto the Lord. Therefore whether we live or die, we are in the Lord."[46] Simplicity is a cleansing of our lifestyle to provide a more clear path for relationship with God and other humans. It is abundantly clear that the more we "have" the more we worry about keeping "it." The less we have the more we can be concerned with our spiritual discipleship. In the parable of the Rich Young Ruler[47] and the text about the purses,[48] we have clear teachings of Jesus for the discipline of simplicity.

FRIENDSHIP

"Iron sharpens iron: and one man sharpens another."[49] We are in need of trusting friends. We are in need of being trustworthy friends. Friendship builds bonds of belonging, love, tradition, trust, and a sense of companionship. Human friendship is a crucible in which the elements of friendship with Jesus Christ are molded. One cannot exist as a Christian without a sense of relationship with others. Not just a relationship with a denomination or a cause, but a flesh and blood relationship with another person.

For men, who are taught, trained, and threatened to be independent, self-sustaining, and not trusting of others, this is one tall order of a discipline. But, nonetheless, we need friendships. In them, we learn to experience love, jealousy, fear, admiration, hope, kindness, homoeroticism, abandonment, and the myriad of other feelings and spiritual complexities of life. Without friendships, we create a world born of our own selfish desires, or, worse, a world of our own neurotic transferences. Theology, and even spirituality of the Christian tradition, has been woefully lacking in coverage of friendship. In part, I believe, because most of our literature is written by white men, who typically write from an academic place of isolation. But Scripture is not so void. In I Samuel we have a very moving account of the friendship between two men: Jonathan and David. Listen to how the author describes their friendship: "When he had finished speaking to Saul, the soul of Jonathan was knit to the soul of David, and Jonathan loved him as his own soul."[50] A non-sexual, loving, and compassionate friendship. A friendship which weathered incredible love and much outside interference. A relationship perhaps not unlike that between Jesus and the Beloved Disciple.

A very real part of daily living, as we shall discuss in greater detail in the next chapter, is that many men exist in a friendless life. Perhaps a wife or roommate is considered "best and only friend." The spiritual discipline we are discussing here is quite beyond this boundary. Every man needs three or four good friends in whom he can confide and be a confidant. In these friendships we rejoice in a living and breathing part of the Kingdom of God. Our fears can be voiced and heard, our loneliness abated, our joys celebrated, our losses mourned, our work and family discussed, and our souls well-held. Here we learn how to be a trusted, spiritual friend.

COMMUNITY

Without question, Christians are called to community. There must be time for all the other disciplines in our lives. There must also be time for us to be in the community. Not the leader or the fringe person, but an integral part of some trusting community. This can be in a cell group in the church, fellowship, a gathering of friends, at formal worship, etc., but somewhere, we need to be a responsible part of a community. In a culture that is very anti-institution and in a period of time when people are hesitant to join anything, this is a particular discipline that is presently under seige. It is easier, and expedient, to be solo, or to only go where we get what we want. But we are not called to such selfishness, we are called to be giving and recieving in a community.

> Now the eleven disciples went to Galilee, to the mountain to which Jesus had directed them. And when they saw him they worshiped him; but some doubted. And Jesus came and said to them, "All authority in heaven and on earth has been given to me. Go therefore and make disciples of all nations, baptizing them in the name of the Father and of the Son and of the Holy Spirit, teaching them to observe all that I have commanded you; and lo, I am with you always, to the close of the age."[51]

On a more intimate level, this means honoring our baptismal covenants and belonging to local communities of faith. Baptism is our ritual of initiation into the community. Lifelong membership, with all its attendant joys and sorrows, is the faithful keeping of that convenant. The community needs to keep discipline just like the individual does. If our churches are not well-disciplined, our communities of faith will be lackluster, visionless, and spiritless. Those who keep the disciplines must likewise keep the community alive and constantly call others to the faith.

SUMMARY

Keeping these thirteen disciplines, and our faith in the presence and power of the Holy Spirit, will help us "keep our bootstraps tight" as we ski down the slopes of life that are often enjoyable, frequently scary, and sometimes just plain dangerous. When we are spiritually prepared, we can meet any challenge of life. It takes work, and these thirteen disciplines offer us some very direct courses of action. The holiness and blessing of which the writer to the Hebrews spoke is, in part, quite present through these disciplines.

It is important to remember that our Christian tradition cautions us about seven sins that will delay, destroy, or seek to subvert our spiritual growth. Each of these sins can tumble us down a slippery slope if we are not fully prepared. Each of these sins can be a powerful force to keep masks on us. The seven are:

- anger
- envy
- gluttony
- greed
- laziness
- lust
- jealousy

In some of our Christian traditions we are more comfortable talking about liberation theology, social justice, or politically correct issues of the day. I caution you to not get carried too far away from the seven sins—seeds of each of them are found in all the hurts and brokenness of our world today. In fact, I would dare say that each has a part in why more of us are not further along in our spiritual growth. It takes discipline to cleanse our souls of these sins. Since we will never be perfect, and are cautioned to not even try for such a thing, we must confess our need for the Holy Spirit. Beyond any discipline we may keep is the power of God's Holy Spirit to sustain, encourage, uphold, forgive, rebuke, direct, and love us. We need the Holy Spirit, for we cannot ever hope to be disciplined or in union with God without it. The gifts of the Holy Spirit help us with the disciplines. These gifts of the Holy Spirit help us take off our masks. These gifts of the Holy Spirit bring us the grace of God. They are:

- love
- peace
- joy
- kindness
- gentleness

- goodness
- faithfulness
- patience
- self-control

These thirteen disciplines—the eight masks, the gifts of the Holy Spirit, and the seven traditional sins—offer us a lot to consider and a wealth of spiritual activity. However, this is what the Christian life is all about. We need to take ourselves seriously, our God seriously, and our part in God's Kingdom seriously. By living these disciplines, we create within our souls a fertile area for the seeds of the Spirit to take hold and grow to good fruit. Now that the disciplines have been discussed and outlined, we have been reminded of the seven sins and the gifts of the Holy Spirit, we are ready to look at the eight masks men wear that keep us from our God-given desires. At the same time, we will explore ways to remove the masks and celebrate the God-given desires hidden beneath them.

Chapter 4

The Mask of Loneliness
Hides a Man's Desire
for Community

But he himself went a day's journey into the wilderness, and came and sat down under a broom tree; and he asked that he might die, saying, "It is enough; now, O Lord, take away my life; for I am no better that my fathers."

— I Kings 19:4

Loneliness seems to be a curse that men pass on to one another from one generation to the next. If there is one common theme I have found in my own life, and constantly present in most men with whom I work, it is the presence of spiritual and emotional loneliness. Because of fear of abandonment or rejection, experience with abuse or violence, lack of role models, or societal pressure upon men to achieve and compete, many men withdraw from any friendships or community. As a result, many men are very, very lonely. To be without a trusted and trusting friends or community is to be isolated from the abundant life for which Jesus lived. To live with a sense of loneliness is to feel outside the circle of humanity, to feel not good enough, to believe that one is unworthy of friendship or love, and to feel estranged from God. It is to feel like Elijah, petitioning God for release of pain. Often, sadly, many men simply accept loneliness as a fact of life.

It is the most basic human loneliness that threatens us and is so hard to face. Too often we will do everything possible to avoid the confrontation with the experience of being alone, and sometimes we are able to create the most ingenious devices to prevent ourselves from being reminded of this condition. Our culture has become most sophisticated in the avoidance of pain, not only our physical pain but our emotional and mental pain as well. We not only bury our dead as if they were still alive, but we also bury our pains as if they were not really there. We have become so used to anesthesia, that we panic when there is nothing or nobody left to distract us. When we have no project to finish, no friend to visit, no book to read, no television to watch, or no record to play, and when we are left all alone by ourselves, we are brought close to the revelation of our basic aloneness and our so afraid of experiencing an all-persuasive sense of loneliness that we will do anything to get busy again and continue the game which makes us believe that everything is fine after all.[1]

Because men are conditioned in our society to be independent and not "needy," men are not directed toward community. It may also be that in order to separate from birth mother, from whom baby boys perceive they are different, males learn how to differentiate, but never learn how to intimately rerelate as individuals. It may be because we rarely move from mother to a loving relationship with father or siblings that we never experience a strong sense of belonging and trust. It may be because of some genetic code of hunters and gatherers that males historically never join in community. Regardless of the causal reasons, all of these factors lead men away from community and toward loneliness. Whatever the causes may be, familial and societal conditioning, jealousy, envy, homophobia, competition (and surely it is a little bit of all of these), many men today are lonely. This loneliness is painful, and because it is, we subdue its impact with so many methods. Work, play, sex, alcohol, TV, and sports are often used to hide the pain of loneliness. So much so that one could say much more energy is spent on the denial of loneliness in our culture than is spent on loneliness itself. Because loneliness is not socially acceptable in our society, men learn to hide it. We do not have any good, sustaining friendships; we are not a part of any nurturing communities, but we certainly do not want it known that we are lonely. So we wear masks to hide our loneliness.

As a boy, my dreams of adulthood were very vague, scary. Being a worried optimist, I had just expected that all would work out all right. It did for Ozzie and Harriet and for June and Ward Cleaver, after all. And so I embarked on the journey, without a compass or a map. Work seemed to be such a good narcotic. So I worked, did well. All too soon a brown-eyed woman entered my life. She said she loved God; she said she loved me. Said she'd be with me forever. I worked on this dream, her dream, also. Another degree, a transfer, kids. . . . I worked on studies, husbanding, fathering, my career—so promising—my family, the car, the garage door, the fescue lawn, my wife's wishes, my bosses expectations . . . I worked. It really was satisfying; the accomplishment, the goal-setting, the achieving. But I found myself forty years old and lonely. I was disconnected from everything, a lamp unplugged . . .[2]

Behind the mask of loneliness hides a great deal of sadness. Men have learned so well how to act and behave as if autonomous and independent that we have become strangers to ourselves. This is the first loneliness—estrangement from our own bodies and souls. Listen to this man quoted above and you will hear his courageous cries to end his painful loneliness, a man well established in society, a father, lover, son, confessing loneliness for community within his own flesh. How many men go their entire lives without ever even perceiving that they can love themselves, not to be independent but interdependent, not alone but in solitude, not friendless but in community? Men will work, perform, achieve, drink, fornicate, abuse, suffer, self-castrate, intellectualize, deny—men will do anything to keep from feeling lonely.

For years I would never be able to sit still or alone at home. When I would get home, if no one else was there, I would turn on the TV or stereo. I would sit and eat or drink beer(s). I could not stand being alone or being in silence. I did not know that at the time. I thought I was just making good use of my time. After all, you are never supposed to just sit, or be alone. I could get work done or entertain myself. Even when I was with my wife, I did not like to be idle. I just wanted to be talking, doing something, or having sex. It was just common sense to stay busy or to have several things going on at once. Often, it was almost as if I was composing myself from the day's events and getting ready to go back out the next day and perform.

When I started speaking with a group of men, I found out I was not the only one who lived like this. Everybody had different ways of avoiding it, but we all were sure lonely. I think one of my biggest fears is to feel lonely. Now I can admit that because now I have some friends. Men friends. Now I like myself and treat myself better. Now I know that I need a community. I also know that I have to be a good friend to others. I need a community and I also have to help form a community for others. I am still catching myself trying to'disappear' from others, or by force of habit putting on the "I'm all alone in this" mind-set; but at least now I know there is more to life.[3]

Too often we wear a mask and do not even know it. Too often we allow pressures of society to keep the mask covering up our faces and souls. This man found that his daily routines were constructed in a way so as to prevent his feelings from being actualized. His work, hobbies, even his sexual patterns were working together to construct a mask behind which he could hide. When he began developing some trusting male friendships, at midlife, these patterns were exposed and his true desire for friendship and community naturally was revealed. It is interesting to note the use of the word "disappear" in this letter. Men are experts at disappearing. We fail to respond when something hurts us; we go away, we disappear. We will not go places where we feel uncomfortable. We say "give me a call," to test and see if the other person really wants to talk to us. When people disappoint us or offend us, we stay away. When the pain is too much, we disappear into alcohol, sex, work, religion, or school.

A second experience that happens long before men have any control over their own destiny is that they are born with anatomical differences that seem to predetermine a course of male loneliness. Anatomically women are born with the capacity to accommodate; they can accommodate vaginally, and they can accommodate in utero, but anatomically males seem to be able to accommodate no one. This early "accident" appears also to have consequential long-term ramifications. In relationships, men seem much slower to accommodate than women. Some men have extraordinary resentments over a woman's ability to nurture inside her a child. Men do not nurture inside, but they do tend to bottle up inside. And men, who are anatomically not accommodating, seem most strongly to express this fact by going through life without friends. Virtually every study done on men and friendships reveals that men rarely have close friendships during their adult lives, except sometimes with their wives, though even that seems to be exceptional. . . . Men learn to be independent and self-sufficient, and men learn to be rugged loners.[4]

One cannot be in community and be disappearing at the same time. One cannot be independent and self-sufficient and in community or union with God at the same time, either. So to drop the mask of loneliness is to be present and appearing at all times, to be part of a real community. When Elijah asked God to take his life, he wanted to disappear from the community. He had enough of fighting the prophets of Baal and of running in fear of Jezebel. He was lonely and he just wanted to disappear. Interestingly, he said in despair, "I am no better than my fathers." Here the great prophet drops the mask of loneliness for a moment and correctly states that this is a generational problem. All too often we simply perpetuate this pain from one generation to the next. But God will not leave Elijah in a state of loneliness. God sends an angel to him, feeds him, and gives him direction. For the man seeking a way out of loneliness, there is no better example. We need to receive the word of God, be fed by God, and take our direction from God. As the disciples saw with whom they walked on the road to Emmaus after they were fed, so too can we see that Christ is with us when we digest God's word. Ultimately, as we learn to exist in human community, we also learn to live within the community of heaven as revealed here on earth. Every other person alive has some message from God for us. Every other person alive has some sense of community to offer us. We have to allow ourselves to be fed this way by God. Men must learn that we need other people, both to reveal God to ourselves and to help reveal ourselves to other people. Today, like Elijah, many men are tired of running from women, or other men; tired of being chased by fear of failure, homophobia, under-employment, and rejection; and tired of running from jobs that suck the very life out of us while we watch the world continue to frag-ment and endlessly spin out of control. Many a man today would like to join Elijah under the tree and exclaim in exhaustion, "take my life, Lord, I'm tired of going it all alone." Yet, as with the great prophet, God will not leave us alone, either. Through Scripture and revelation, through Sacrament and rite, through ritual and liturgy, we are fed well by God. Through Christian community, we can hear about, learn about, and experience the love and mercy of God.

The issue of personal boundaries in the movement from loneli-ness to community, is an age-old concern for those involved in spiritual growth. The question is best joined during early medieval mysticism and the work of St. Bernard of Clairvaux (1090-1153). He was concerned with the union of the Christian individual with Christ the Bridegroom. He saw as the final and most definitive act of spiritual love the union of the believer with Christ. When this occurs, the "soul is transported out of itself" and the human becomes one with God. St. Bernard compared this event to drop-ping a drop of water in a lot of wine where it will lose its own identity and become like the wine. For him, the communion of believer and Christ can occur when the believer thus "loses" his soul into the will of God, momentarily. For him, then, one would lose the truest sense of one's self in relationship with God. Building upon his work in the later Middle Ages, German mystic Heinrich Suso (1295-1366) further identified this union:

> Like a being which loses itself in an indescribable intoxication, the spirit ceases to be itself, divests itself of itself, passes into God, and becomes wholly one with Him, as a drop of water mingled with a cask of wine. As a drop of water loses its identity, and takes on the taste and colour of wine, so it is with those who are in full possession of bliss; human desires influence them no longer; divested of self they are absorbed in the Divine Will, mingle with Divine Nature, and become one with it.[5]

There is no loneliness in community. Alone, one may be in solitude, but the community will be in one's soul, sustaining him.

One's boundaries are fluid enough to allow a sacred ebb and flow of others within one's midst. There is no loneliness in union with God. Human community prepares us, simultaneously, for community, or union, with God. As St. Bernard and Suso write, we are united. Jesus says it this way: "The one who finds his life will lose it, and the one who loses his life for my sake will find it."[6] When we move from loneliness to community, and to union with God, at its most mystical peak, we are moving from "not knowing the self" to ultimately "giving up" the self in love. This is no quick or easy journey. St. John of the Cross's definition (see Chapter 3) of the "dark night of the soul" is most applicable here. Community, and union, are the ultimate joys of human living, but come with attendant suffering and fears to reach them.

For many men, community with other men and community (union) with God are unnatural, and unknown. They are the opposite of everything men are taught and raised to do and believe. Community, however, is a better way to experience the heights of the Christian experience. Loneliness means isolation from other people, and also isolation from Jesus Christ as personal Savior. This is simply no way to live. For a man to be closer to union with Jesus Christ, to hope to be a drop of presence in the Eucharistic wine, thus gaining sacramental value, we must come out from behind our masks of loneliness and expose what is behind them; the God-given desire to be in community. Loneliness is not a fact of life, it is the Egypt for many men today who need to be freed from its bondage and led into the Promised Land of community: *with one another, and with God.*

DISCUSSION QUESTIONS

1. What did this chapter mean to you?

2. What is loneliness like for you? Give examples.

3. What do you do to avoid loneliness? Give examples.

4. What biblical men do you identify with in your loneliness?

5. What masks do you wear when you are lonely?

6. Describe your experiences of community.

7. Tell about the joys you know of community.

8. Which Christian disciplines help you move from loneliness to community?

   —in an active sense

   —in a passive sense

   —in a sensual way

   —in a spiritual way

9. Which of the seven traditional Christian sins keep you out of community?

10. How are the nine Christian gifts of the Holy Spirit active in removal of this mask?

Chapter 5

The Mask of Rage and Anger Hides a Man's Pain and Hurt

He went up from there to Bethel; and while he was going up on the way, some small boys came out of the city and jeered at him, saying, "Go up, you bald head!" And he turned around, and when he saw them, he cursed them in the name of the Lord. And two shebears came out of the woods and tore forty-two of the boys. From there, he went on to Mount Carmel, and thence returned to Samaria.

—II Kings 2:23-25

"What is the emotion or emotions you most typically associate with a man today?" I will generally ask at retreats or programs about men. Without fail the singular answer is "anger." When I seek more description, the participants will say such things as:

- Well, we all know what men are capable of.
- Cross a man and you'll pay for it.
- Most men are always angry or always covering it up.
- I never upset a man because I don't know what will happen.
- Men don't discuss their anger; they pout and sulk.
- I've seen too many men break things when they are angry.
- My father always hit me when he was angry.

Surely we can generalize and say that how to express anger is often a problem and a challenge for men. If we look at the childhood of many, if not most, males, we will find that anger was not an acceptable emotion. Young males are told to not show their hurt, not express their pain, to work outside of themselves, to produce and to perform, to compete against all others (particularly other males), and never to disappoint Mother. Just sit back and imagine getting some, or all, of these messages as a child. Wouldn't you grow up into someone who is a little bit angry and raging? For some men there has pretty much been no other route left.

Recently, I watched a family at the beach. There were Mom, Dad, a preteen daughter, and two toddlers—a boy and a girl. The two youngest were doing what most children do at the beach, digging in the sand by the water's edge. Typically a sand castle or sand mountain is built to withstand the power of the incoming tide. The little boy and girl were busy with their work, side by side, for many minutes. Their little castles were really nothing more than little mounds of scooped-up sand. Eventually a wave came in and pushed the sand away and leveled their work. This cycle was repeated about three times. The little boy began to yell and clench his fists, shaking them at the sea. The little girl looked at him, paused, and began digging again. Is there a way men are wired in life that causes us to select rage and anger as a natural response? Certainly the girl in this event was more politically correct today, but were both simply following a genetic predisposition for a response to a very frustrating situation? I do not have the answer, nor will anyone else. So this is a dilemma for us, how to deal with male rage and anger, which probably is both inherited and socially conditioned.

Elisha, the great prophet, son of Shaphat, was renowned as a healer. After receiving the mantle from Elijah, Elisha performs such miracles as purifying the water at Jericho,[1] multiplying the widow's jar of oil;[2] the restoration of the Shunammite's dead son to life;[3] purifying the spoiled pottage and multiplying the twenty loaves;[4] and the curing of the leprosy of Naaman.[5] It is particularly noteworthy to remember the previously quoted verses about Elisha's treatment of the young boys who mocked him. Even the great prophet was unable, at one time, to control his anger. The one who revived a stranger's young boy had forty-two boys killed because they made fun of his baldness. Is it inherited, or is it taught? We do not know. But we do know that all humans, no matter how famous or healing, can also be filled with murderous rage. The entire nation was so spellbound by the recent O.J. Simpson trial, in part, because Americans do not seem to believe that everyone has the same emotional makeup and capability. Scripture makes it clear, however, that we all have the same emotions; we just process them differently for a variety of reasons. It is typically taught and preached in the church that Elisha was the prophet who succeeded Elijah and who performed many miracles for God. We need, however, to also teach and preach Elisha as a man so consumed with rage and anger that he murdered these boys. When we only portray one aspect of personality in biblical people, humans today are quite apt to see themselves as hopeless sinners and far removed from the true humanity shown in the Bible. Jesus wept; Jeremiah cried; David lustfully sinned; Gehazi lied; Peter questioned; and so forth. These people had many of the same qualities you and I have today. Only Jesus was perfect—no prophet or person alive today will be. Elisha is no less a profound prophet for this act; the young boy I saw on the beach is no less a boy because the ocean defeated his efforts. Nonetheless, today our society demands from men perfection, performance, production, no open displays of emotion, and no weakness and success in competition. Men are angry and enraged because of it.

There once was a young boy who moved with his father to Richmond, Virginia. His parents were recently divorced and this seven-year-old was moving to this new and big city with his dad. Because his dad worked and he had not made friends yet, the young boy had many free hours of time. From the window of his home, he could see the statue of the famous statesman and general of the South, Robert E. Lee, which had been cast with the Confederate hero riding upon his horse. So well-known was the General, in fact, that the statue only bore one brief inscription title upon its base—"LEE." Eventually the young boy was allowed outside the home as he became more familiar with this neighborhood. He became fascinated with the statue and spent countless hours there playing and imagining himself in battle. This statue was the good friend of a lonely boy. After about a year, the boy and his father had to move to a new city. Knowing his son was so attached to the statue, and knowing the move would be difficult for his son, the dad took his boy to the statue to have a final farewell picnic before they moved. As they were leaving the statue for the last time, the boy looked at his father and said with some surprise, "Gee Dad, I never got to know the name of the man riding on Lee."

When we do not tell our stories—our full stories—much is lost. When we just talk about the rage and anger of a man, and not about a man's sadness and hurt, we have left out the most important part of the story. When we only focus on a man's use or misuse of his anger, and do not invite, allow, and encourage a man to feel sad and to hurt, we have helped the man lose his true identity. There is not a single occasion when someone is angry or raging that sadness and hurt are not fueling the emotion or action. Beneath the mask of rage and anger is the feeling of pain and hurt. Elisha was pained and hurt by those boys. Sadly, he did not claim his hurt; rather he lashed out in rage. The young boy at the beach did not feel his pain at having his work destroyed; he was angry at the entire Atlantic Ocean. The full story of a man is that we are hurt every day, we are living with a great deal of pain every day, and we have little experience and little encouragement to name it, experience it, or live with it well. So, with great justification, we mount up on our horses of anger and rage and we ride them instead. Men mount great political battles, great military battles, great workplace battles, great family battles, great marriage battles, all the while feeling a clarity of mission and justification, despite the risk to themselves or others. A man's anger can ride him into so many battles, under flags of great purpose, day after day. But if the rest of the story were known, would these battles occur? If a man were able to, or invited to, or had some experience in feeling and expressing his pain and hurt, would so many battles occur? Definitely not.

Let's go back to some of the messages parents, teachers, preachers, or our entire society can give little boys:

- Oh, shut up, be a man, and don't cry.
- Suck it up and get out there and try again.
- Stop whining; it doesn't hurt that much.
- Only a girl would act like that.
- Stop pouting and finish it.
- Oh, just come on and do it; I had to as a kid.

It's as if pain and hurt have been ripped from the dictionary of life for boys, and so as grown men those same boys only have rage and anger left to them. Why? Because underneath these emotions are pain and hurt, and these two powerful feelings have been denied access to our consciousness. As men learn and experience the reality of feeling pain and confessing hurt (physical, psychic, spiritual, emotional, sexual, etc.), their levels of anger and rage will diminish, almost as if by miracle. This is no small task, however, because everything in our society runs counter to taking the time and effort toward allowing full expression of these emotions for men. Unfortunately, it is more "manly" to react in rage and anger than it is to confess hurt and pain. John Wayne, Rambo, Clint Eastwood, and even Fred Flintstone never sold a show or movie titled *Real Men Show Pain* or *Let Me Tell You About My Sadness*.

Our belief here, however, is that it is more spiritually sound and more faithful to Christ to publicly and privately confess our pain and hurt than it is to lash out in rage and anger. Recall the account in Luke's Gospel of Jairus and his daughter. She was near death when Jairus, a ruler of the synagogue, came to Jesus and asked for help. Jairus was hurting and he was in pain, and he reached out to Jesus for help. This is a sign of good masculine spirituality. Jairus teaches men today how to be directly open to their deepest wounds and care for their souls, and thus for others. Rather than rage at the world or storm off in anger, he surrendered in his pain to Jesus. For those who demand immediate results, and answer to action, this is a truly wonderful text. For those who want to see the power of Christ in action, this text is invaluable. For men who want a way out of endless nights of holding on to decades of anger and rage, this is a very liberating text.[6]

This text illustrates the difference between stopping at the surface with anger and rage and plummeting the depths of our souls to find the blessings of expression for sadness and hurt. In verse 52 we read that "all were weeping and bewailing her." Unlike Elisha who denied his hurt and lashed out in a rage, Jairus confessed his hurt and appropriately wept. For men today, the loss of boyhood innocence, the sacrifices made to please others, the ways they have tried to conform to societal expectations for us, the loss of children in their homes after divorce, the stress of employment, the scars from war in strange lands, the death of beloved spouses and children, the inability to feel their own sense of belonging, loneliness, lack of true male friends, compulsions and addictions to food, alcohol, sex, work, worry—all these and more are invitations to men to confess pain and hurt. Like Jairus, today's man needs to weep and wail, loud and long. I have heard so many men say "I haven't cried in fifty years," "Crying is a waste of time," or "Being sad only shows you can't take care of yourself." My ears hear this, but my eyes see men just filled with pain and hurt. Too many of us, too many times in our lives, are totally out of inner focus. We deny, ignore, work away, swear away, drink away, or do whatever it takes to avoid our own pain.

Almost ten years ago a man who was involved in my upbringing, and for whom I always had great admiration and affection, died. Upon hearing the news, I instantly distanced myself from my memories of good feelings and responded with something like "Oh yeah, gosh, how about that. . . ." I remember deciding in that moment to not show my true sadness to anyone, for after all, this was a man whom I had not seen in a decade. It was not until recently when I talked about him with some friends that I realized how sad I was about his death, and how much I missed him. I suddenly started to cry and could not stop for about thirty minutes. This wave of sadness was absolutely startling to me, but I learned through it how truly hurt I was by his death. Somewhere within me was a little reservoir of hurt, occupying a place that nothing else could, until it was expressed. Now, I have a freshness and sense of acceptance of his death. I have a new-felt joy in remembering all our times together, something I had not done in—you guessed it—about ten years! I was angry that he died, so I just ceased to remember him or our relationship with any closeness or intimacy. But, thank God, the hurt never left, and now, after draining the reservoir of hurt, the issue is resolved within my soul. From the kind of quiet inner anger I experienced here, to the hateful and raging anger of those who murdered fellow citizens in Oklahoma City in 1995, to the misdirected anger and rage of rapists, pouters, corporate raiders, gossipers, greedy men, men with controlling life-styles, men who through their daily living are blaspheming God, or to those who exploit the earth, we can see the damage done by so much unexpressed hurt and pain. A few more tears and a little less false machismo would do our world a wealth of good!

Had Elisha thought to himself, "Gosh, it sure hurts when they make fun of my baldness" and quietly consoled himself, or shared the hurt with a friend, or if he had told the boys he did not appreciate their malicious words, forty-two lives would have been spared. Taking off our masks of anger and rage to reveal our pain and hurt is that serious. I am not saying that sometimes anger and rage are not justified; there are events in our lives where anger and rage are very much the appropriate responses. Rather, this is a call to fruitful expressions of these emotions, and a call to be aware of the feelings that often fuel our anger and rage. This is an invitation for us to the spiritual discipline of surrender to God's love and to prayerfully remain a full part of the Christian community. Because there is such a societal taboo for men against expression of hurt and pain, this may be the most difficult mask of all for men to work at removing. But we are not without direction.

The man God consecrated in his mother's womb to be a prophet to Israel, Jeremiah, son of Hilkiah, is a wonderful guide for the man seeking to remove his masks of anger and rage. Jeremiah is delivering prophecy to the people about their faithlessness. Rather than strike out with military strength or political acumen, he weeps and mourns for the violations of the covenant between God and Israel. Surely many a pastor today has had these same feelings as the priest for God, as have many Christians among the laity. Jeremiah said:

> My grief is beyond healing, my heart is sick within me. Hark, the cry of the daughter of my people from the length and breadth of the land: "Is not the Lord in Zion? Is her King not in her?" "Why have they provoked me to anger with their foreign idols?" "The harvest is past, the summer is ended, and we are not saved." For the wound of the daughter of my people is my heart wounded, I mourn, and dismay has taken hold on me. Is there no balm in Gilead? Is there no physician there? Why then has the health of the daughter of my people not been restored? O that my head were waters, and my eyes a fountain of tears, that I might weep day and night for the slain daughter of my people![7]

Jeremiah was angry at their sinning and violations of God's love; he was enraged at their stealing, murder, Baal worship, adultery, and false swearing. The people said "peace peace" and Jeremiah knew there was none. And so, he wept. He expressed, in word and action, his pain and hurt. As a prophet, he called the people to tears as well. He rode into town upon a horse named sadness. He was a proud and victorious leader, whose full story would be told. Because of his powerful prophecies, born of tears, for Israel there was a period of restoration. In fact, Jeremiah saw restoration as a natural result from expression of pain. In the book of restoration he wrote of the people: "with weeping they shall come, and with consolation I will lead them back."[8] That is, God will restore those who come to God with weeping, with true sadness and hurt in their souls, and God will be their God. Rather than be solely responsible for our own lives, or "man enough" to take care of ourselves alone, the Christian is invited to turn, with weeping and gut level expressions of pain, to God our Sustainer.

Psychologists say that a man's anger is often rooted in his feelings of inadequacy or fears of castration. "Saving face," a cherished male commandment, may also be read to mean, "save manhood." And no man wants to be without manhood (to be castrated). But our true salvation rests in fully experiencing ourselves as created and sustained by God. Our manhood is not saved through anger or rage, but rather in faithful keeping of our covenants with God. As did blind Bartimaeus, the Ethiopian eunuch, or Peter on the sea and Moses at his call to mission, we need to turn to God with our needs, and we will be answered. From the brokenness in our world, to the difficulties in our daily living, to the hurts in our own families and personal lives, there is a wealth of pain and hurt that God is waiting to heal for us.

The author of Lamentations stated this so well:

My eyes flow without ceasing, without respite
until the Lord from heaven looks down and sees;
my eyes cause me grief at the fate of all the maidens of my city.
I have been hunted like a bird by those who were my enemies
without cause; they flung me alive into the pit
and cast stones on me; water closed over my head,
I said "I am lost."

I called on thy name, O Lord, from the depths of the pit;
thou didst hear my plea,
"Do not close thine ear to my cry for help!"
Thou didst come near when I called on thee;
thou didst say, "Do not fear!"
Thou hast taken up my cause, O Lord,
thou hast seen the wrong done to me, O Lord,
judge thou my cause.[9]

DISCUSSION QUESTIONS

1. What did this chapter mean to you?

2. What are rage and anger like for you? Give examples.

3. What do you do to avoid rage and anger? Give examples.

4. What biblical men do you identify with in your rage and anger?

5. What masks do you wear when you are raging and angry?

6. Describe your experiences of pain and hurt.

7. Tell about the joys you know of pain and hurt.

8. Which Christian disciplines help you move from anger and rage to expressing pain and hurt?

—in an active sense

—in a passive sense

—in a sensual way

—in a spiritual way

9. Which of the seven traditional Christian sins keep you from expressing pain and hurt?

10. How are the nine Christian gifts of the Holy Spirit active in removal of this mask?

Chapter 6

The Mask of Compulsions
Hides a Man's Desire for Love

Now the whole earth had one language and few words. And as men migrated from the east, they found a plain in the land of Shinar and settled there. And they said to one another, "Come, let us make bricks, and burn them thoroughly." And they had brick for stone, and bitumen for mortar. Then they said, "Come, let us build ourselves a city, and a tower with its top in the heavens, and let us make a name for ourselves, lest we be scattered abroad upon the face of the whole earth."

—Genesis 11:1-4

The essence of a compulsion is that we want to make a name for ourselves. Here, in an early account from the creation text, humans are already busy trying to establish for themselves unity, fame, and security. They discount the love and generosity of God the Creator and begin to compulsively build a testament to their own egos. In a very real sense, they have declared themselves unloving and unlovable, as they have set out to "make a name for themselves." You can almost picture these formerly nomadic people scurrying about trying to collect the material to make the brick, tending fires, and finding ways to build this huge tower. There must have been so much confusion, so many attempts at one design or another, and so many opinions offered that the task was almost overwhelming. But, they committed themselves to their task and were driven to accomplish their goal, so much so that God's attention was brought upon them. Seeing that they were consumed with this selfish and destructive desire, God humbled them out of love.

There was a man who had a slight obesity problem. He went to a doctor who advised him to do two things. First, the man was to eat only fruits and vegetables, no meats, no high sodium, or high-fat foods. Second, the man was to begin an exercise program. Both of these lifestyle changes were to begin immediately. Well, these were some very significant changes for this man. He was accustomed to a very couch potato-type lifestyle, and he enjoyed steak, ice cream, and desserts. But he was determined to take better care of his body, so he followed the doctor's recommendations. One month after the initial visit he returned to the physician. "My goodness," the doctor exclaimed, "you look wonderful." Indeed the man had lost about fifteen pounds and did look very good. "How did you do this?" the doctor asked. The man replied that he was determined to succeed and he had strictly followed the orders given him. "I ate only fruits and vegetables, particularly the leafy green type, and I drank plenty of clear liquids. I did not snack and I did not waver from the routine." "Wonderful, wonderful," the doctor exclaimed, "and what did you do for exercise?" "I climbed the walls!" the man replied.

This sense of exasperation is more common than one might imagine in our culture. Not just from dieters, but from all of us when we have lost our spiritual balance. The amount of alcohol abuse, prescription and illegal drug abuse, overwork, over volunteering, endless sexual performances, food and dietary problems, limitless shopping excursions, and total consumer-oriented attitude in our society is clear evidence that as a people we compulsively seek to fill gaping holes in our souls. The perceived void of love creates these holes that we feel, whether we are consciously aware of it or not. When we stop and look around, we see a society that is "climbing the walls" trying to find love. Just as the Israelites at Babel, we have forsaken God and we are building testaments to our own desire, trying to make "names for ourselves." The compulsive drive in American culture to have the best clothes, the most expensive homes, the finest cars, a TV and VCR in every conceivable place, private schools for the children, fancy parties, exotic vacations, or any visible sign of success and value possible is quite obvious to the naked eye. What is not so obvious, but nonetheless very present, is the hunger that drives these compulsions—the hunger for love.

In creation, through the word and action of prophet and apostle, in Bethlehem and at Golgotha, God promised and delivered to us his love. Through our own sinfulness, dullness, disbelief, or whatever, we continue to doubt and reject this gift. Instead, we choose to look for love in human terms, in ways that meet (at least temporarily) our own needs. Often the same is true in our human relationships. Someone does love us, but we convince ourselves it is not true and off we go in a never-ending search, building towers of testament to ourselves, and climbing walls of frustration. The people could not wait and he could not wait, so Aaron built a golden calf, compulsively seeking ultimate love.[1] David decided to possess another for his own lustfulness and pride, so he compulsively demanded sexual relations with Bathsheba, and then sacrificed her husband.[2] Amnon decided that he would take what and who he wanted, even claiming that he was "so tormented he became ill" (early Hebrew for "climbing the walls" with lust?), when he raped his own sister, Tamar, and conspired with his family to degrade her. His compulsion to fill the void within his soul was to be filled with her flesh, a tragic consequence of his unmet desire for love.[3] The Prodigal Son parable delivers to us a heartbreaking story of a man who is compulsively driven to hurt himself with wine, women, and gluttony, all while the love of his father awaits his return.[4] This compulsion is seen with Ananias and Sapphira, who, when asked to contribute to the disciples' work, compulsively lie and seek to selfishly hide their prosperity, loving money more than the Lord and the community.[5] In his letter to the church at Galatia during his third missionary journey, Paul quite plainly declares the difference between compulsion and love. He writes, "But I say, walk by the Spirit, and so not gratify the desires of the flesh. For the desires of the flesh are against the Spirit, and the desires of the Spirit are against the flesh; for these are opposed to each other, to prevent you from doing what you would."[6] The balance between our desires and living in the Spirit is crucial, for in the balance is where love lives. So that we do not misunderstand his point, Paul lists for us the works of the flesh and the gifts of the Spirit. Listed here for us, it is plain to see the compulsive nature of the first category and the love that celebrates life in the latter. Our task is to balance the two, while accepting the mercy and forgiveness of God in our daily living.

Paul's Desires of the Flesh

- fornication
- impurity
- sorcery
- licentiousness
- enmity
- strife
- jealousy
- anger
- selfishness
- discension
- party spirit
- envy
- drunkenness
- carousing

Paul's Gifts of the Holy Spirit

- love
- joy
- peace
- patience
- kindness
- goodness
- faithfulness
- gentleness
- self-control

Recently, I went with my family to the Portsmouth Invitational Tournament in Virginia. This is an annual event featuring men's college basketball athletes competing for the NBA draft. College students from around the country are invited there to show their talent to NBA scouts who may not have seen them play live during the year, in hopes the student will be drafted to the pros. During the games the stands were absolutely filled with enthusiastic fans eager to see such high-caliber play at a local court. Tables completely surrounded the basketball court. At these tables sat the pro-team scouts, a total of 165 in all. They had before them books of college career statistics on the athletes, that they read while watching the games and the players. It was somewhat obvious that this event was a real "meat market." Only a few, if any, of these players would receive contracts, transforming them from college athletes to millionaires in the professional ranks. So the players were here to perform, and the scouts were here to judge. This makes for a very pressure-filled event. For males, this is a rather typical experience, though usually more mundane. We are what we produce. We are what we perform. We are rewarded or denied depending upon our production and our statistics. We are used to this type of lifestyle, whether we sell insurance, work with computers, teach, preach, are a lawyer, doctor, or mechanic. As men, we are scouted and rewarded for our life's statistics.

It follows, then, that we would have little experience of unconditional love, the type of love God offers. It follows, too, that we would have little experience of human love without conditional strings of performance attached. In fact, if you reread Paul's lists for the desires of the flesh and the gifts of the Spirit, the first list seems much more familiar to males and the latter much less familiar. Being only as good as our statistics, or being only viewed as a competitive performer leads naturally to a lot of "fleshy" activity. Unaware and inexperienced in receiving and giving love, we will be unfamiliar with satisfying our hungers with the fruits of the Holy Spirit. So the mask of compulsions is usually worn, and men try to fill the inner void with money, sex, power, jobs, homes, cars, degrees, titles, etc. Beneath the mask, however, is still the desire for love, for a taste of those holy fruits, for peace, joy, goodness, gentleness, and the rest.

"Just as I Am Without One Plea" is a great hymn, isn't it? Think of it—"just as I am." This is pretty much counter to any experience of mine, except after surgery. Our lives as men are consumed and controlled with compulsive doings. And if we stop, if we truly seek unconditional love, we need be prepared for a host of trouble. Try going to a meeting and having no report. Try going home and not working around the house. Try going to a party and having no project, volunteer activity, or special work event to talk about. Our society forces compulsive behavior on us. We are conditioned, and fully expected, to be busy climbing the walls with this, that, and the other thing going on. And all too often, we buy into this mentality. The Lord, however, says to stop and open the gifts given to us through the Holy Spirit. Simply stop. No tower building, no making a name for ourselves, just stopping, and accepting that who we are is good enough. Through the spiritual disciplines of prayer, surrender, friendship, and silence we do find avenues toward this gift. In fact, the Holy Spirit's gift to us of self-control can be the first one we need to open, getting divine help to stop living compulsively and start living in love. The choice is ours to make.

The mistakes of Aaron, David, Amnon, the Prodigal Son, and Ananias and Sapphira can be very instructive to us. There is another way. Even after his brothers had deceitfully plotted his death and betrayed him, Joseph chose the gift of self-control and loved his brothers.[7] The Psalmist reminds us how important the gift of patience is with these words, "I wait for the Lord, my soul waits, and in his word I hope."[8] Jeremiah writes about the gift of kindness that God gives to his people in the period of restoration, "I will be their God and they shall be my people."[9] Paul very plainly teaches us about love in his letter to the Corinth church, leaving no doubt that the spiritual aspect of love transcends any strings we might try to attatch.[10] Paul yet again writes in love, and about love, in his letter to Philemon. He brings together the balance of flesh and Spirit here, lovingly pleading for freedom for Onesimus. In verse 16 Paul writes, ". . . no longer as a slave but more than a slave, as a beloved brother, especially to me, but how much more to you, both in the flesh and in the Lord."[11]

What Paul writes to Philemon really balances well the whole point of this chapter. We can live and act in love both in the flesh and in the Lord. What the men's movement and many contemporary writers have identified for us, however, is that too many men live with lives out of balance, most typically toward the flesh. We live this way not out of ignorance or conceit, but out of roles defined for us by genetics and culture. With the gifts of the Holy Spirit to help us, we can change and move closer to the Christian way of love. It may take suffering, as in the life of St. John of The Cross; it may take a dramatic transformation as happened to Saul; it may take the gentle guidance of another as the Ethiopian eunuch learned from Philip, but conversion from a compulsive lifestyle to a life of love is certainly possible. At Pentecost, God gave us the opposite of Babel, one language, a common understanding, and one spirit. With this new unity through Christ Jesus, you and I have all hope and sustaining encouragement to seek and receive love.

DISCUSSION QUESTIONS

1. What did this chapter mean to you?

2. What are compulsions like for you? Give examples.

3. What do you do to avoid compulsive behavior? Give examples.

4. What biblical men do you identify with in your compulsive behavior?

5. What masks do you wear when you are being compulsive?

6. Describe your experiences of love.

7. Tell about the joys you know of love.

8. Which Christian disciplines help you move from compulsive behavior to love?

   —in an active sense

   —in a passive sense

—in a sensual way

—in a spiritual way

9. Which of the seven traditional Christian sins keep you away from giving and receiving love?

10. How are the nine Christian gifts of the Holy Spirit active in the removal of this mask?

Chapter 7

The Mask of Performance
Hides a Man's Desire for Acceptance

He also told this parable to some who trusted in themselves that they were righteous and despised others: "Two men went up into the temple to pray, one a Pharisee and the other a tax collector. The Pharisee stood and prayed thus with himself, 'God, I thank thee that I am not like other men, extortioners, unjust, adulterers, or even like this tax collector. I fast twice a week, I give tithes of all that I get.' But the tax collector, standing far off, would not even lift up his eyes to heaven, but beat his breast, saying, 'God, be merciful to me a sinner!' I tell you, this man went down to his house justified rather than the other; for every one who exalts himself will be humbled, but he who humbles himself will be exalted."

— Luke 18:9-14

I spent the first eighteen years of my life in Lansdowne, Pennsylvania. This was, in the 1950s to 1970s, a typical American community, one square mile in size, with about 13,500 residents. We were a border town of Philadelphia, so we had some good influences and people, for the city mixed into the community. One aspect of the community from which the residents benefited greatly, and eventually I did, too, was our local volunteer fire company and rescue squad. Long before the Commonwealth required advanced training for the volunteers, the Lansdowne Fire Company had an excellent program in place. When I was a young teenager I joined the company, and spent several years in training and duty with fire and rescue apparatus. I was able to learn a great deal through this activity, much that has been valuable to me in later life. I was also able to give of my time to a community that was important to me.

Now I live in Elon College, North Carolina, 600 miles from Lansdowne, and am obviously no longer involved in the fire company, although I keep an active membership through dues. Last summer, the Lansdowne Fire Company celebrated its one-hundreth anniversary. Those of you living in towns with volunteer fire companies will recognize this as a fairly significant event to be celebrated. A large parade with over 125 fire trucks from surrounding communities and several states was planned along with a whole day of festivities. I decided to go back for the day and enjoy the activities. While there, I was asked to help direct the fire trucks down a wide street to a place where they would be judged for awards. This was a great deal of fun for me because I got to see every truck and talk with the crews as they prepared for the parade. After twenty years or so of no involvement, I had a front-row seat. It was a great experience. After several hours all the trucks and equipment were judged and it was time for the parade. As I mentioned previously, the town was one square mile. Let me clarify: it is big enough to hold about 120 fire trucks. Every street had these huge vehicles lined up and ready to go. There was literally no room for local traffic or much movement until the first trucks began to move. Many of the surrounding towns had sent several trucks to the parade in hopes of winning prestigious awards and money. After going through the judging areas, most of these trucks got separated from one another. For the parade, they had to be back together.

After the judging, my job was done. I was walking down a street toward the parade route. Suddenly, a fire truck pulled up next to me and the driver asked me where a certain street was, so he could drive there and meet the other trucks from his town. He recognized me as the guy who had directed him earlier. What he did not know was that I had not lived there for over twenty years and had no idea where most streets were located. I thought as hard as I could and then told him where I thought it was. This fire truck drove off, as big as a tractor-trailer, weaving its way through very cramped conditions, following my directions. I continued along my way. I cut down an alley and two or three blocks, coming out near where I wanted to watch the parade. Behind me I heard air brakes stopping a truck. I turned around to see the fire truck I had directed earlier, still quite lost. This time they demanded directions and made some comments not usually directed to clergy. Fortunately a police officer was there and he gave them exact directions. As they drove away, one of the firemen leaned over to me and sarcastically said, "It's pretty bad when the people who live here don't even know the right direction."

As Christian men, the church is our hometown. As Christian men, the word of God provides a map of direction for living in our home neighborhood. And, yet, I believe that not too many of us know our way around well enough to give much direction to others, let alone to ourselves. We live in the community of the blessed and the forgiven, the redeemed and the sustained, yet we get so lost. Sometimes we don't even have to be gone for twenty years; we simply have no direction right where we live. One area that shows our lack of direction is in our drive to perform. We are told to perform, want our cars to perform, our computers to perform, our wives to perform, our children to perform, our animals to perform, our equipment to perform, our bodies to perform, our minds to perform . . . it is as if we are only as good as what and how we perform. Halls of honor are even built and revered as testaments to performance. In our society, ultimately, a man is only valued by how he performs. Paycheck, work product, awards, titles, degrees, all these are allegedly signposts for "how good a man" one really is: perform, perform, perform. When we buy into this mind-set, which is most of the time, we have lost all direction in our hometown. Even the church bears responsibility here. Every year at annual conferences we give awards to the churches that have the greatest increase in membership, the greatest increase in stewardship, and the most gifts to special causes. We don't award churches who are overflowing with faithfulness and zeal in the Spirit, rather, we recognize the ones who have "performed" according to secular standards. The hometown direction is even lost in the church.

The two men in Luke's parable quoted at the beginning of the chapter are quite instructive in this matter. We find one man who is totally performance-oriented, "Lord, Lord, look at me, look how I perform. I'm not like the others . . . no, not me. Look how well I perform. I fast, I tithe, I'm no tax collector, etc." (perform, perform, perform . . .). Then we find the other man who is total humility and acceptance-oriented. "Lord, be merciful to me, a sinner. (I'm OK)." In fact, the word "justified" in verse 14 of the text means "accepted by God," this one was accepted in his humble contrition without having to perform anything. He was in his own spiritual hometown and very able to read the word of God as a directional map. How many times have any of us, clergy and laity, put down our performances before God and simply presented ourselves as sinners seeking mercy? Even seminary is a place where one must perform. Society and the church have lost their direction when it comes to the acceptance we receive from our God when we stop trying to earn our salvation. To be humble, as in verse 14, is to accept freely given grace, confessing that nothing we do will earn or merit reward from God. We come before God just as we are; needing to perform nothing.

David, the son of Jesse, volunteered to go and fight the champion from Gath, a Philistine named Goliath, in a competition between the two countries. David was a young man, the youngest son of his father, and no warrior. But, nonetheless, he volunteered to represent his people in this battle. Since no other Israeli volunteered, Saul accepted David as his peoples' warrior. Listen to this exchange between David and Saul as Saul prepares David for battle with Goliath:

> Then Saul clothed David with his armor; he put a helmet of bronze on his head, and clothed him with a coat of mail. And David girded his sword over his armor, and he tried in vain to go, for he was not used to them. Then David said to Saul, "I cannot use these; for I am not used to them." And David put them off.[1]

Saul tried to put all these battle armaments onto David, and David refused them. Certainly Saul meant well; he wanted to protect the soldier, but David was uncomfortable with the bulk and weight of the battle gear. He took it off and went with what he was used to, himself. History records that young David, alone and untested, went into battle with only his own cunning and swiftly defeated the Philistine giant. David took nothing special into battle, he accepted his own ability. The same is true for men today. We do not need to wrap ourselves up in armor of performance to do battle with life, we only need to bring ourselves and our faith. We do not need to throw caution to the winds and offer ourselves as hapless victims. What we do need is to confess we cannot defeat the giants of life—greed, lust, gluttony, laziness, anger, pride, and envy—by outperforming them and earning God's grace. We defeat them by accepting God's grace and living responsible lives. The blessing that Saul gave David, "Go, and the Lord be with you" is the only thing we need to accept and carry with us in life.

Many of us spend our entire lives, our personal energy and professional endeavors, trying to perform for approval. It may be approval from God, a mother or father, peers, wives, friends, co-workers, lovers, or siblings, but nonetheless many of us endlessly continue in the pursuit. Many of us have also found this pursuit to be filled with disappointment, depression, confusion, and great sacrifice. The treadmill of chronic performance has worn down many a soul. Even though God has given us a good map, we are lost to the gods of performance. The spiritual discipline we need, then, is to "accept acceptance" from God and live liberated lives of Christian joy. To do this, we need to accept as foundational that God loves us and we are good enough just as we are. Then, we can competently and judiciously meet the demand of our lives. It is again a matter of selection and priority. God will be merciful to all of us sinners. Paul makes this very point in his letter to the church at Rome:

> The word is near you, on your lips and in your heart (that is, the word of faith which we preach); because, if you confess with your lips that Jesus is Lord and believe in your heart that God raised him from the dead, you will be saved. For man believes with his heart and so is justified, and he confesses with his lips and so is saved. The scripture says, "no one who believes in him will be put to shame." For there is no distinction between Jew and Greek; the same Lord is Lord of all and bestows his riches upon all who call upon him. For, every one who calls upon the name of the Lord will be saved.[2]

DISCUSSION QUESTIONS

1. What did this chapter mean to you?

2. What is it like for you to always have to perform? Give examples.

3. What do you do to avoid performances? Give examples.

4. What biblical men do you identify with in your drive to perform?

5. What masks do you wear when you are performing?

6. Describe your experiences of acceptance.

7. Tell about the joys you know of acceptance.

8. Which Christian disciplines help you move from performing to acceptance?

   —in an active sense

   —in a passive sense

—in a sensual way

—in a spiritual way

9. Which of the seven traditional Christian sins keep you away from giving and receiving acceptance?

10. How are the nine Christian gifts of the Holy Spirit active in the removal of this mask?

Chapter 8

The Mask of Control
Hides a Man's Desire for Friendship

Then Herod, when he saw that he had been tricked by the wise men, was in a furious rage, and he sent and killed all the male children in Bethlehem and in all that region who were two years old or under, according to the time which he had ascertained from the wise men.

—Matthew 2:16

The Massacre of the Innocents is perhaps one of the most tragic accounts in history of one man's desire for control over other human beings. Herod was concerned that he was about to lose military and political power because of the birth of the infant boy Jesus in Bethlehem. What the prophets had said long ago was now coming true and the people of Israel had a savior born to them. Herod lied to the wise men and told them to locate and bring the boy to him, that he might worship him. The Magi knew this was untrue so after visiting the Christ child with Mary and offering their gifts, they "went home another way." In a "furious rage," Herod ordered the execution of any boy under two years of age in the region, figuring that the infant Jesus would be executed in this general bloodbath. Tragically, mass execution took place. Herod was so driven to control, so determined that his role not be threatened, so fearful of a potential challenge from this one baby boy, that, when he could not locate him, he had all baby boys massacred.

Joseph was sold into slavery because his brothers were jealous and wished to control him.[1] The Pharoah exerted tremendous control over an entire nation out of greed and malice.[2] King Ahab stole

89

Naboth's vineyard because he simply wanted to control the land, regardless of what this action meant to Naboth and his family.[3] After learning that his master turned down the riches, Gehazi went after the commander because he wanted to control those precious elements, even if it meant lying to Elisha.[4] Peter betrayed Jesus because he would rather control his own destiny and control the fate of his own flesh than confess his Lord and risk persecution.[5] The people decided that what Stephen was preaching was an indictment of them. Rather than repent and change, they chose to control the messenger by killing him.[6] In his letter to the church at Corinth, Paul reminded the people that they did not control the signs of the kingdom, but that control of spiritual matters was God's dominion, something which was problematic to Jews and Greeks.[7] From just these few examples we see that Scripture is faithful to the reality of the human drive to control. These are some rather dramatic accounts of controlling behaviors. Most of us are a little more subtle in our controlling behaviors, perhaps even unaware of them, but we are all controlling at one time or another. When we are controlling, we are not in friendship, for friendship is a relationship of equality. Friendship can only exist when each person is seeing and being seen clearly.

When I was a young boy, our family spent many summer vacations living in a cottage on the banks of the Brandywine River in Chadds Ford, Pennsylvania. One of my favorite memories was of my father taking us to the Brandywine Raceway in nearby Delaware to watch the horse races. For me it was a wonderful adventure to travel to and sit in a very exciting atmosphere. I even did, on occasion, double my allowance! The horses all wore black blinders, covering their view of anything to the side as they raced. I asked my dad what those black things were on the sides of the horse's face, and he explained that they were to keep the horse's eyes strictly on the track in front of it and not on any distractions to the side, for things beside the horse might scare it. So, the horse went through the race, and much of its life, with blinders on, totally in the dark as to what was around it.

Very often, you and I spend a lot of time wearing blinders, oblivious to what is occurring right next to us. We go through life focused upon the race in front of us, running and running toward some goal line. We completely miss what is right next to us. In our efforts to control our own destiny or control the lives of those near us, we put on blinders and run as fast as we can in one direction. (Sometimes it may even seem like someone is riding on our backs, spurring us on.) Next to us, and all around us, there exists an entire world that we never even see. Herod had blinders on when he ordered the execution of the baby boys. Ahab had blinders on when he stole the family vineyard from Naboth. Saul had blinders on at the execution of Stephen. I had blinders on until after my surgery experience. Some of them came off a bit and a whole new experience of daily living was revealed anew to me, as were certain individuals. We each wear blinders in our daily lives, certainly more than one set, that block us from good vision of reality. It is our desire to control our environment, our destiny, our friendships, even our God, that puts these blinders around our eyes.

When we begin to take our blinders off, we see the masks we have been wearing. When we wear masks of control, we cannot have true friendship with any other person, or Christ. When I always have to be right, first, best, paid the most attention, consulted, the one who sets plans and directs everything, the one who always gets his way, the one who never loses, the one who is never found at fault, the one who never needs help, the one who never asks for anything, the one who is always in charge, I am wearing a heavy mask of control. And who wants to be around someone who always has to have control? It may look good in old Western movies or hypermacho flicks, but in real life, a healthy relationship includes a very permeable wall of being and relating, which we call friendship. Particularly in our relationship with Jesus Christ, if we are so much in control in our lives, how can we ever allow ourselves to be saved by Jesus, or to be open and vulnerable enough to seek the mercy of Christ?

To take off our blinders and remove the mask of control is no small order. Most of boyhood is spent hearing and trying to comply with family, society, and church messages to be in control. Boys are taught to be in control of their emotions, their playthings, their relationships, their very destiny in life. Watch any playground activity today: When a little girl is hurt, she will get comfort from peers and the teacher. A little boy will be told to get out there and try again. The little girl will be allowed to cry; the little boy will be quickly reminded boys are tough and do not cry. Even in 1995 our society is carrying these messages. When programs aired on television the past year or so about the men's movement and certain retreats where men gather and often cry and grieve, many people asked me if I went on these "crybaby" trips. I was told, "God, what a bunch of wimps." There is precious little reinforcement today for men who want to shed the mask of control, which could also be called pseudocontrol, because usually behind the mask is one scared and frightened person; one lonely person. Imagine thinking that you are so in control that you are autonomous and you need no one. Unfortunately, many men have been taught this enough that they believe it. But, truth be told, behind this mask is one lonely little boy in the body of a man. To remove this mask, to keep the mask of control off, and to keep the blinders off, we need to be a friend and have a friend. No control is not the same as out of control or irresponsible. We are each responsible for ourselves, but not in a tightly wrapped isolation-type way. Without getting lost in semantics, a good question is: Do I have friends? Are there other people I can go to, in particular, other men, and share my true self? Do I have male friends in which to share my masculine experiences, and to whom I am available to hear their stories? Am I only talking to my wife, or to a bottle, or to some vague inner voice, or are there real live men who are my friends with whom I can discuss my joys, fears, failures, successes, hopes, ideas, marriage, work, parenting, etc.?

"Iron sharpens iron; and one man sharpens another."[8] In friendship, we "sharpen" one another, we help bring a creative and loving edge to the human experience. Control and isolation lead to dullness and ambiguity; friendship leads to clarity and vitality. Recall, for instance, that when Philip befriended the eunuch, the Ethiopian man suddenly was converted and sought baptism in the faith.[9] Friendship gives us an emotional and spiritual connection to the human and the divine. For men, because of our training in control, honest, life-sustaining friendships with other men are rare. In fact, many men seem to collect female friends, where we secretly join with them in belittling those "other men" who are insensitive and the like. We do not venture out into honest friendships with other men—friendship beyond sports, work, cars, and civic associations. Other issues such as homophobia, competition, fear of the unknown, father fears, time pressures, and quite frankly, women's mistrust of when men are together, are all forces that keep us apart. The desire for male friendship, however, does not go away. It longs for exposure from under the mask.

My own experience is perhaps quite similar to yours. After high school, I went away to college. Any friendship from elementary school through high school was suddenly severed. I never have made an effort to contact anyone from my hometown, unless I see them in the normal course of my travels. Somewhere I got the idea that "real men" do not need male friends, and a "real man" would never call an old friend just to rekindle the friendship. The same pattern was repeated after college. In seminary and denominational training I was told that ministers were professionals and thus could not expect to be in friendship with church members beyond the necessary formalities. I secretly always wondered why I was lonely. I decided that something was wrong with me, or that wanting close male friends was too feminine a desire. I let the loneliness live within me, mask on, blinders in place, tightly controlling my life.

In 1990 I had had enough and I responded to an article in a newspaper for a local men's group, one of the first to come out of the men's movement. There, in our first meeting, were eighteen men from this area, gathered in one room, for no other purpose than to explore life as a man. I should probably say eighteen very nervous men. But, much to my surprise, as we introduced ourselves, I was in the majority with feelings of loneliness and lack of clarity as to what being a man meant. Our group is still together, now, with nine men meeting weekly. We try to take a weekend retreat together every year and expand the friendships as we so desire in and outside of the group. Over the years each group meeting has been unique. We are each significantly different men from when we began our group. Issues and concerns addressed over the years have included love, admiration, anger, mistrust, rage, confessions of guilt, forgiveness, marriage and family issues, work-related issues, sexual concerns, and financial concerns. Through it all, we have grown together as friends who are committed to one another as Christian men. We do not allow alcohol, sex, drugs or macho bull at the meetings. These times are committed to learning how to remove the masks of control and become friends. There is a myth that all women know how to be good friends. There is also a myth that men do not want to have good male friends. Many women do not have a clue as to how to be a friend; many men desire close male friendships. I will give testimony that I want and need close male friends, that I want to be a close friend to other males. In this men's group, and in a male clergy group of which I am a member, I have met my need. Meeting this need has given new life to my emotional and spiritual well-being. I have a renewed vigor in my marriage and parenting, and a wealth of vitality at my work. Interestingly, I have noticed my needs to be controlling diminish as these friendships have increased.

I never heard about friendship in all of my years of theological training. I memorized many definitions of love, many great theories of God's relationship to humankind, but nothing about friendship as a theological or spiritual term. Theological training, and most white-male theologians, stand mute on the point. Why? Probably, because they were writing from behind a mask with blinders on in a detached and academic way. I am not ridiculing their efforts. But isn't Christian faith empty if we do not have flesh and blood experiences of intimacy? What the men's movement has said to the church is "put some flesh on your theology," and so we must. While theology may have been traditionally silent, Scripture is not. The mask of control must be taken off if we want to truly celebrate Christian friendship.

"When he had finished speaking to Saul, the soul of Jonathan was knit to the soul of David, and Jonathan loved him as his own soul."[10] I know of no more beautiful illustration of male friendship than this biblical statement. Read the verse again and ponder what has been written. Can you feel it in your own soul? Two men who love each other so much their souls are "knitted" together as one, loving each other as they love themselves. Truly, this is male friendship. As men, we need one another to "sharpen" our souls. Societal expectations are very restrictive for men seeking friendship. We need help processing the negative messages out and the message of Jesus Christ into our lives. Some men seem to form friendships naturally, while others seem to need more formal ways to meet, such as with weekly group time. There is no right or wrong way, but here is the need to be met. Jonathan and David are quite instructive to us, as are the disciples themselves. These were twelve men, who sometimes were good friends, and who sometimes doubted, betrayed each other, or broke off into subgroups. As men, we hate rejection and abandonment. As in Paul's letter to Philemon on behalf of their mutual friend Onesimus, we can be tenacious in tendering relationships and seek to hold others accountable, out of love. Men are too often quick to let friendships dissolve over trivial matters, because we are hurt. Scripture is teaching us that friendship takes effort, and includes some pain, but the pain of hurt is far less damaging to our souls than the pain of living behind a mask of loneliness.

> David rose from beside the stone heap and fell on his face to the ground, and bowed three times; and they kissed one another, and wept with one another, until David recovered himself. Then Jonathan said to David, "Go in peace, forasmuch as we have sworn both of us in the name of the Lord, saying, 'The Lord shall be between me and you and between my descendants and your descendants, for ever.'" And he rose and departed; and Jonathan went into the city.[11]

DISCUSSION QUESTIONS

1. What did this chapter mean to you?

2. What is it like for you to always have to be in control? Give examples.

3. What do you do to avoid control? Give examples.

4. What biblical men do you identify with in your desire to control?

5. What masks do you wear when you are performing?

6. Describe your experiences of friendship.

7. Tell about the joys you know of friendship.

8. Which Christian disciplines help you move from control to friendship?

   —in an active sense

   —in a passive sense

   —in a sensual way

   —in a spiritual way

9. Which of the seven traditional Christian sins keep you away from giving and receiving friendship?

10. How are the nine gifts of the Holy Spirit active in the removal of this mask?

Chapter 9

The Mask of Producing
Hides a Man's Desire to Just "Be"

All the congregation of the people of Israel moved on from the wilderness of Sin by stages, according to the commandment of the Lord, and camped at Rephidim; but there was no water for the people to drink. Therefore the people found fault with Moses, and said, "Give us water to drink." and Moses said to them, "Why do you find fault with me? Why do you put the Lord to the proof?" But the people thirsted for water, and the people murmured against Moses, and said, "Why did you bring us up out of Egypt, to kill us and our children and our cattle with thirst?" So Moses cried to the Lord, "What shall I do with this people? They are almost ready to stone me."

—Exodus 17:1-4

In our society it is quite safe to say that a man is primarily valued for what he produces. A man cannot just "be." A man must prove himself with outward production. The story is told of two fire hydrants located at opposite corners of the same intersection in a large city. Both of these fire hydrants are functional, but the city fire department only ever uses one of them. Because of the nature of this neighborhood, there are frequent calls for the fire department; they are probably called here eight times a month. Now, the first hydrant, on the south-side corner, is very old. It is somewhat tilted into the cement, the cement is cracked around it and crabgrass is growing through the cracks. The reflective paint on this hydrant is all but gone, one hydrant cap is gone, the other hangs there useless because the threads are stripped. This hydrant is a favorite for the neighborhood dogs. The second fire hydrant is located on the north side of the corner. If there were such a magazine it would be the centerfold for *Fire Hydrant Monthly.* This hydrant can be seen from blocks away by the fire personnel because it is upright in the ground, totally covered with reflective paint as well as easily identifiable reflective tape. This hydrant is surrounded by gleaming flat sidewalk which is bordered by landscaped lawn. All the caps are on this north side hydrant, and if a dog should even come near it, a neighbor chases it away. The outward appearance of this hydrant is showcase quality.

Every time there is a need for water from a hydrant at this intersection, the city fire department truck is connected to the same hydrant, no matter which side of the street the fire is on. Which hydrant? The one on the south side of the intersection. Why? Because the fire department knows what the city water department knows. Underneath the ground, where the water main pipes are connected to the hydrants to deliver water, the south side hydrant is connected to a sixteen-inch main and on the north side of the intersection the hydrant is connected to an eight-inch main. The sixteen-inch main delivers four times the volume of water to its hydrant than the eight-inch main across the street. What is visible above the sidewalk reveals nothing about the source beneath the surface.

What is on the surface is often shiny and new and attractive and showy, even politically correct. But what counts is what is beneath the surface, delivering life to that which has the outward appearance. In discussing masculine spirituality in American culture, this is a very important point. Our society is very appearance-oriented. Social and political correctness in America today has a great deal to do with surface looks. Just take a quick look at television and print media advertising. If we believe these people then all that matters is soft hair, straight teeth, facial clarity, belt size, and the odor from our armpits and shoes. There is little in our society today that encourages the sacred art of plumbing the depths of one's soul, or establishing friendships and community life centered upon spiritual patience or "beingness." We are what we produce and how we appear. Jesus Christ, however, does not care for the surface performance. Jesus Christ cares about the sacred flow of holy water in our souls beneath the surface.

The people were ready to attack Moses because he did not perform to their expectations. They anticipated freedom would be easy and apparently believed their leader could provide for all their needs. When some hardship occurred, they were ready to stone him. He could not produce, so he would suffer for it. It is as if they already read the book of James and decided that faith without the resulting good works, i.e., Moses producing water, was not enough. Moses, the spiritual leader and liberator of the people, was of low regard when he could not continue to produce miracles and immediate results. Perhaps today's pastor can take some comfort when held personally responsible for church incomes and membership stability or growth—ours is not the first generation to seek production and disregard faithfulness. When I meet someone who does not know my occupation, and later learns that I am a local church pastor, it is almost 100 percent guaranteed they will ask me, "So, Reverend, how big is your congregation?" As a male, I am dimly aware that this is a significant question on several levels. It ranks right up there with clergy competitions to have the biggest "steeple" in the conference. The underlying message here is "if your produce enough, you will have a large congregation." Ministers of small churches, like people who live in small homes or drive small cars, are somehow just not quite up to snuff in our culture. We are, particularly as males, what we produce.

If performance is *how* we do it, production is *how much* of it we do. For men in America, that better be a lot. When I completed my Doctor of Ministry so many people said to me, "Well, I'll guess you'll be leaving Lynnhaven Colony for a big church now." It was kind of shocking to realize that this church was not considered a good enough place for me. In fact, I've gotten some questions about "when are you moving?" from friends at home, as if my failure to be in a bigger church invalidates my calling or my degree. I think the subtle message is that, as a man, if I produced well enough, I'd surely be on Main Street somewhere now. This is not just true for clergy. I have friends who are lawyers and they tell me that each week they are held accountable for every half hour of the workday, to make sure it is a "billable" half hour. Then, every week, a meeting is held to read aloud and have in print before the entire staff everyone's billable sheets. There is no concern for compassion, client nonlegal needs, or the lawyers' family—just the income produced. Really, what occupation is there that does not demand we produce or we move on? What would happen in your workplace if you began to be more concerned with peoples' welfare and souls, as Christ called us to, instead of the final rate of production? I doubt the results would be very satisfactory. Unfortunately, this produce-or-else mind-set has also prevailed in the church and in the spiritual life of many Christians, to the point where we are always concerned with producing results. Concern with visible results and ignoring the mystery of the Holy Spirit is just the opposite of how we grow spiritually in Christ.

Christ calls us to a "beingness" of our faith, not a "producing-ness." As men, we are always taught to produce. When the size of our production reveals how much of a man we are, this becomes a very startling message. The Bible is not silent on this issue, however, and it is made clear that Christ is not calling production specialists. Jesus is calling faithful human beings. For example, when God called Moses, the shepherd's response was one of being. "Here am I."[1] Naaman, commander of the Syrian army, had contracted leprosy. He went for healing to Elisha who told him to simply dip himself seven times in the River Jordan. This type of nonproducing beingness was foreign to Naaman. Enraged, he wanted to produce healing his own way. But Elisha again told him he had nothing to produce; he simply had to be dipped in the Jordan seven times, "Go and wash in the Jordan seven times, and your flesh shall be restored, and you shall be made clean."[2] Convinced by his people that he did not have to produce anything or earn his recovery, Naaman simply went to the river as he was, and he was healed.

The prophet Isaiah makes it quite clear that humankind can produce nothing toward our own salvation, but salvation alone comes from the Lord. We must simply be grateful recipients. "Comfort, comfort my people, says your God. Speak tenderly to Jerusalem and cry to her that her warfare is ended, that her iniquity is pardoned, that she has received from the Lord's hand double for all her sins."[3] Luke presents an equally compelling spiritual message of beingness with one verse "Lord, be merciful to me a sinner."[4] Nothing to produce, nothing to do. Just "be" in a state of humility and surrender to God. In Paul's letter to the church at Ethiopia the point is delivered quite well. Paul writes:

But God, who is rich in mercy, out of the great love with which he loved us, even when we were dead through our trespasses, made us alive together with Christ (by grace you have been saved), and raised us up with him, and made us sit with him in the heavenly places in Christ Jesus, that in the coming ages he might show the immeasurable riches of his grace in kindness toward us in Christ Jesus. *For by grace you have been saved through faith; and this is not your own doing, it is the gift of God—not because of works, lest any man should boast. For we are his workmanship, created in Christ Jesus for good works, which God prepared beforehand, that we should walk in them"* (emphasis added).[5]

The message from God says, that we need to be grateful recipients of life itself, not nonstop producers seeking to earn salvation.

In the summer of 1994, I was repainting the outside of our house. On one particular day I had reached a point near the peak of the roof where the power lines connect to the house. I had called the Virginia Power Company three weeks earlier to arrange for a lineman to be there that day to temporarily cut-off the power to our house, so I could safely paint around the wires. To be sure someone would be there from the power company I also called the day before and reconfirmed the request. Everything was prepared. But, by 12:00 noon on the day I needed them, the power company had not arrived, even though our appointment was for 10:00 a.m. at the latest. After waiting in the hot sun, I called the power company and the dispatcher assured me the driver was enroute. By 1:00 p.m. no one had arrived. I left my ladder up and the paint outside, and I went up the street to 7-Eleven for a Big Gulp and the newspaper. Since my daughter's school was letting out at 2:00 p.m. this day, I went to get her. We returned home by about 2:15; there was no power company line truck in sight. I was angry. This was my last day off from work and my last daytime chance to paint around the wires. Soon our doorbell rang and I went to answer it. There stood the power company lineman. I was ready to complain sarcastically to him when he said, "Well, how do you like it?" "How do I like what?" I asked. "Come look," he said. I went outside and looked up at the house, and to my astonishment, the paint job was complete. "You weren't home, and I know which wires not to touch, so I just finished it for you," he said. I was totally surprised by such an act of generosity and kindness. It was an unearned and unexpected gift. This power company employee, on a hot day, had climbed my ladder and painted the side of my house, out of his own sense of responsibility and community. In fact, he made me inspect the painted area rather thoroughly because he was very proud of the job he did. Without expecting anything in return, he smiled and drove away.

This generosity, this compassionate kindness, this gift, was given the same way God gives us grace and mercy—as an unearned surprise that changes our life and warms our heart. I had to do nothing for this man, and I produced nothing. I just existed, and I received a gift from him. As Paul wrote, this was "not of my own doing," but simply a freely given gift. My anger, my impatience, my sarcasm melted instantly when I saw the painted wall. In the letter to the Hebrews it is written ". . . be content with what you have. . ."[6] I think I now know what this means. I know I am closer to Christ when I can just "be." When I can just exist and not be in such a rush, busy trying to earn salvation, hurrying to do five things at once, or complaining about the inefficiency of other people. When I can just be still, I see, hear, and feel the presence of the Lord. When we, as men, can silence the voices that tell us we must always be producing something, we are the sum of what we produce, and real men produce measurable results. We will hear the Lord. Still waters run deep.

Too many times we all are called by God, our names are spoken, and yet we attend to earthly voices. We try to please fathers and mothers, teachers and preachers, employers and employees; but we fail to try and please God. We are so busy trying to produce results for others here, that we fail to be still and know God. Rare is the occasion when we just "be," and say to God, "speak, for thy servant hears."[7] The Scriptures are clear, however, that a lifestyle of "being" is a most appropriate way to live. Jacob learned at the Jabbok that his wrestling would produce nothing, he had to simply be still and receive the blessing, "Your name shall no more be called Jacob, but Israel . . . ."[8] Moses was being faithful, and heard the Lord without having to produce anything; "Here am I."[9] In the call of Joshua we can discern that he produced nothing to earn this blessing; it was a freely given gift he simply needed to receive, "Moses my servant is dead, now therefore arise, go over this Jordan, you and all this people, into the land which I am giving to them, to the people of Israel."[10] The cycles of accounts about the great prophets Elijah and Elisha in I and II Kings show over and over again that it is not what they produce, but rather how they listen to God and "be" faithful. The prophet Job, after suffering great trial and tribulation, is humbled to know that only being a servant is pleasing to God.

> I know that thou canst do all things, and that no purpose of thine can be thwarted. Who is this that hides counsel without knowledge? Therefore I have uttered what I did not understand, things too wonderful for me, which I did not know. Hear, and I will speak; I will question you, and you will declare to me.[11]

He has learned that there is no need for burnt offerings or right prayers or holy action, just a need to "be" faithful enough to listen to God, and to "see" God. In the Psalms we find ample language of "beingness." Perhaps the most clear passage is this:

> Have mercy on me, O God,
> according to thy steadfast love; blot out my
> transgressions. Wash me thoroughly from my
> iniquity, and cleanse me from my sin . . .
> . . . Behold, thou desirest truth in the inward being,
> therefore teach me wisdom in my secret heart,
> Purge me with hyssop, and I shall be cleansed
> wash me and I shall be whiter than snow.
> Fill me with joy and gladness, let the bones which
> thou hast broken rejoice.
> Hide thy face from my sins, and blot out my iniquities.[12]

It is not what is on the surface that matters. It is not what we produce or how we look. It is how well we attend to the sacred flow of God's love within our souls. Just as Naaman, we are often convinced that we must do many difficult things or do things our way to produce results for ourselves to be good enough for God. But, as the Psalmist writes, all we need is a sense of wisdom to understand the blessings of humility. This is why, in Psalm 116, the author can offer up such a clear voice of praise: "Return, O my soul, to your rest; for the Lord has dealt bountifully with you."[13] The Gospel of Matthew is very straightforward on just this issue. In Jesus' Sermon on the Mount, we hear a clear proclamation toward ending a producing mentality and living a faithful "being" lifestyle:

> Therefore I tell you, do not be anxious about your life,
> what you shall eat or what you shall drink, nor about your body,
> what you shall put on. Is not life more than food, and the
> body more than clothing? Look at the birds of the air;
> they neither sow nor reap nor gather in barns,
> and yet your heavenly Father feeds them.
> Are you not of more value than they? And which of you by
> being anxious can add one cubit to his life?[14]

Obviously the Hebrews who were plotting against Moses had not heard these words, and they were extremely anxious. But you and I have heard them, uttered directly from the mouth of our Savior. You and I are called to not be anxious about worldly things, to not worry all the time, and to not seek to save ourselves. We are called, as the birds of the air, to "be." To be grateful recipients of God's gift of creation. Clearly this is directly opposed to the American dream for males who are to be living, breathing, production machines. But it is directly accurate for the Christian call to faithfulness. Paul writes,

> The word is near you, on your lips and in your heart (that is, the word of faith which we preach); because, if you confess with your lips that Jesus is Lord and believe in your heart that God raised him from the dead, you will be saved. For man believes with his heart and so is justified, and he confessed with his lips and so is saved.[15]

It is almost too "simple" for us to comprehend. As men, we will have to work very patiently and diligently to accept this grace. In our faith, this may be as stunning to us as I was stunned by the kindness and goodness of the power company lineman. But let us make no mistake about this mask. If you are spending your life producing things, making things outside your own body and soul, competing and stacking up results, this may win you reward with an employer, but it is of no purpose in your faith. Christ cares for the inner man, for your soul, for how well and consistently you can "be" a person of faith. This is not a call to laziness or a shutdown, but a call to spiritual balance in your life. The tension between active and passive is most clearly pronounced in this mask. We must "actively be passive" to "be" and not produce. We all certainly have to produce enough to survive, but the balance here is to know the difference between survival and excess. I know that after my surgery, when I could not even roll over in the bed without assistance, when I could produce nothing, was the most spiritual time of my life. Other survivors of trauma, prisoners of war, the disabled, and those who have lost spouses or jobs have said the same thing. Suddenly, when we have nothing and can do nothing about it, we recognize how dependent we are on God. When, sometimes, all we can do is "be," we experience that in God's kingdom, this is enough.

> The Lord is my shepherd, I shall not want; he makes me lie down in green pastures. He leads me beside still waters, he restores my soul. He leads me in paths of righteousness for his name's sake. Even though I walk through the valley of the shadow of death, I fear no evil; for thou art with me, thy rod and thy staff, they comfort me. Thou preparest a table before me in the presence of my enemies; thou anointest my head with oil, my cup overflows. Surely goodness and mercy shall follow me all the days of my life; and I shall dwell in the house of the Lord for ever.[16]

DISCUSSION QUESTIONS

1. What did this chapter mean to you?

2. What is it like for you to always be producing? Give examples.

3. What do you do to avoid producing? Give examples.

4. What biblical men do you identify with in your desire to produce?

5. What masks do you wear when you are producing?

6. Describe your experiences of "being."

7. Tell about the joys you know of friendship.

8. Which Christian disciplines help you move from producing to being?

—in an active sense

—in a passive sense

—in a sensual way

—in a spiritual way

9. Which of the seven traditional Christian sins keep you away from giving and receiving a sense of beingness?

10. How are the nine gifts of the Holy Spirit active in the removal of this mask?

Chapter 10

The Mask of Competition
Hides a Man's Desire for Humility

And James and John, the sons of Zebedee, came forward to him, and said to him, "Teacher, we want you to do for us whatever we ask of you." And he said to them, "What do you want me to do for you?" and they said to him, "Grant us to sit, one at your right hand and one at your left, in your glory."

— Mark 10:35-37

Performance is the rating or judgment given to how we complete a task or do something. Production is how much we do or make by a measurable amount. Competition is the structure within which we produce and perform against other people. Whether we like to admit it or not, a large part of our lives is given to competition. I do not just mean in the gymnasium, either, for competition occurs in marriages, the family, amongst co-workers, friends, churches, and varying ethnic groups. History has shown that some of our greatest military or political conflicts as human beings have, at their core, competition for land, natural resource, power, world influence, and money. We compete when lives are at stake. We compete when careers are at stake. We compete when others' welfare is at stake. We compete when only our fragile egos are at stake.

We even compete in the church. Don't most churches keep a close eye on the membership number, building size, financial endowment, local and national influence, and number of congregations in other denominations? James and John, the sons of Zebedee, are not the only two church folks to want a special seat in the church or in the kingdom. Nor is their mother,[1] the last mother to try to push her sons along in front of others in a competitive way. The gospels are truly wonderful to include this text because once again the humanity of the disciples shines through. Imagine asking Jesus, behind the backs of the other ten, for an extra special seat in his Kingdom.

Think about it. How much time in your life is spent in competition? Where we work, how much money we earn, where we live, the house we live in, the car we drive, the vacations we take, the people we call friends, the church to which we belong. Somewhere in all our decisions about these matters is some competition with others in the community. These decisions include our self-esteem and our feelings of self-worth, both of which are greatly influenced by "how we are doing" compared to others. From church meetings to PTA to civic leagues to Boy Scouts to the military, when we belong to something or give our name and energy to it, we want it to be very favorable when compared to other like groups or individuals. The balance here is between healthy competition, where the goal is sharpening our edges or growing in discipline, and unhealthy competition, where jealousy, envy, and self-righteousness blind us to the common good.

Last year my daughter and I went to see a live filming of the popular television show *Wheel of Fortune*. The owner, Merv Griffin, was doing a salute to the military, so the show was being filmed aboard the aircraft carrier USS *Eisenhower* at Norfolk Naval Shipyard in Norfolk, Virginia. We were among seven hundred pre-ticketed people who were to witness the live recording of two shows. At the gate before the carrier, the military police separated us by ticket group: contestant, VIP, and general. We were in the VIP group of forty people who were taken as a group into the waiting area aboard the ship. This waiting area was below the deck, sealed off from everything else by huge curtains. About ten minutes before airtime the rest of the audience was brought into this room, and then together we all went into the next hangar deck for the show. We were locked in this area for about two hours during the taping. About ten minutes before it was to end, I led my daughter down the aisle and across the hangar to the area where we had come in. I did not want to be caught in this mass of people trying to get off the ship through one tiny exit walkway. The large fire door we had come in was closed and sealed. I asked a guard how we could get out ahead of the crowd. He pointed all the way back across the audience to just where we had been seated. The exit was back over there. Now we were truly going to be last.

I explained to the guard that we wanted to be first off ahead of the crowd, and he kind of shrugged his shoulders and said, "OK, you can go out there," pointing to a small door. We quickly went through the door, sealed it, turned around, and found ourselves in a tiny room with just one door on every wall. No markings, no signs, no nothing. Suddenly the door opposite us opened, several crewmen entered this room, sealed the door, turned and went through the door we had just used, and said nothing to us. Not knowing what else to do, we went through the door they had just come through. Lo and behold, it was a bigger room with a door on every wall! In a growing state of exasperation and some fear, we chose another door, went through, and sealed it behind us. Now we were in a hallway with a door at the far end only. We hurried through that door and found ourselves in the hospitality suite for the show hosts, Pat Sajak and Vanna White. Everyone came to attention and the crew chief offered us refreshments. It was tempting and very humorous, but we wanted to leave, and I saw daylight through a door behind the serving table, so out we went—finally.

In my drive to compete against the other people and get out ahead of them, I got us woefully, and perhaps even dangerously, lost. I was so filled with desire, like James and John, to be first, that I went off with no preparation and no forethought as to the consequences. Just to save us about a fifteen-minute wait! It was quite humbling to be in room after room and to have no idea which way to go. We were lost in the center of an aircraft carrier with no possible way to get out, because of my desire to be first.

Cain and Abel fought against each other and competed in a very deadly game. Because of the jealousy and rage in their competition, Abel was murdered.[2] Jacob competed with his brother for the blessing of his father, aided in his deception by his mother, to the point where their lying and deceit destroyed the family.[3] The laborers competed with one another out of greed in the householder's presence because they wanted wages according to their differing lengths of service.[4] Simon thought that to possess the Holy Spirit (which the apostles had) he could become a more famous and wealthy miracle worker, defeating all his competition. He offered money to the disciples to purchase the Spirit, ensuring defeat of all his competition.[5] Paul was very aware of the danger in unbalanced competition when he wrote to the church in Rome. "Why do you pass judgment on your brother? Or you, why do you despise your brother? For we shall all stand before the judgment seat of God. . . ."[6] The great evangelist was well–aware that envy, jealousy, strife, and enmity had beset the people, one against the other. Competition in excess is spiritually harmful.

I play racquetball regularly with a friend of mine. We have very intense, competitive games in which we both play the best we can to win. We have been doing this for over five years now, one, two, or three times a week. There have been numerous benefits to this, among them the spiritual disciplines of friendship and body self-care. But I have also learned that we both can be very competitive. Fortunately, we are able to talk things through and accept one anothers' behaviors. It was not always this way. For one period we stopped playing together because we were both so competitive. However, over time, we could discuss it and then get back to playing. On occasion we will yell at each other or hotly contest a point, but then we will not leave the court until we have an agreement and we both can honestly state we are not upset. Our competition now is not so much with each other as it is with ourselves, to be the best player we each can be. In fact, we even joke about some arguments in the past and tease each other about being competitive. When I lose, I'll say, "Hey, whatever; it's just a silly game." When I win, particularly several games in a row, I'll declare racquetball a good standard for what a winner I am in life. Once the jealousy, anger, and envy of our competition is openly discussed, the fun has begun, and has stayed.

But issues of competition for men are not always this easy in life. It is rare that at a church meeting, business meeting, employer-employee discussion, spouse argument, or discussion with a family member or friend that a man can disagree, even mildly, and work the entire matter through to mutual closure. Because we are, at our core, very sensitive and loathe to lose (and all relationships eventually have some competitive edges where someone wins and someone loses), disagreement often is denied, avoided, or discounted. For us as men, in particular, competition seems to involve not just how well we do but literally "who we are." To lose is to lose face, even more so, to lose manhood, which has very specific horrifying attributes for a man. So we often compete to save manhood or to reaffirm manhood. We will do anything we can to not lose because at a certain level it is a very castrating experience, something few men welcome. This is why men who are victims of crime, prisoners of war, in lower economic jobs, or unable to clearly express their needs in life will run the risk of chronic poor self-esteem and depression. For most men, to lose in competition to another person, male or female, is potentially a castrating experience. So, as men, we welcome competition as a place to win, as a place to at least openly try to win, or a place to, unfortunately, chronically lose and reinforce our self-loathing. By competing we also get to wear our other two masks, performance and producing, hiding our true selves even deeper behind false fronts.

What does the mask of competition cover? The answer is our God-given desire to be humble. Humility like that which Jacob learned after competing with the angel all night, and his own name was changed.[7] Humility like Moses expressed when he told God he could not speak well enough to the Israelites, confessing an inability to complete a task and asking for help.[8] When Gideon was called by the angel of the Lord to help his people compete against the people of Midian, Gideon was humble enough to know he needed help: "Pray, Lord, how can I deliver Israel? Behold my clan is the weakest in Manasseh and I am the least in my family."[9] In one of his many speeches on humility as a spiritual discipline, Jesus reminds the people who the true "winner" is in competition: "He who is greatest among you shall be your servant; whoever exalts himself will be humbled, whoever humbles himself will be exalted."[10] This is just "flat out" opposite of the message American culture gives to men. What advertisement have you seen recently that boasted for a man that he would really be a "man" if he was the servant of another? Humility and manhood do not go well together in our culture, but they do in God's Kingdom. This is why, for instance, former President Jimmy Carter as a hammer-toting volunteer with Habitat for Humanity is so peculiar to many politicians and to many Americans. But he is quite understandable to a Christian. A true spiritual disciple is not a live-or-die competitor, but a faithful and humble servant. Remember Saul (Paul), a powerful and fanatic persecutor of Christians? After God humbled him on the road he was transformed to the faith. It took that much humility to awaken him. He was humbled even further as a man to be blinded and unable to find his own way. It was Ananias who had to take him by the hand and lead him along the way to new vision.

Today, men need this same type of humility to stop our persecutions of God's kingdom. We also need this same type of humility to allow ourselves to be led by the hand by other Christians who can help show us the way. There is a popular joke, sad in part because it is true, that men will never stop on the highway to ask for directions. We just drive faster. Recall the joke about Moses: The only reason the Israelites were lost in the desert for forty years is because Moses would not ask directions. We don't ask because we do not want to appear needy. We don't want to appear needy because that is less than manly. We don't want to be less than manly because that means we have lost the competition. It is an affront to our existence as a man, a psychic and spiritual castration. This, of course, is to be avoided at all cost. On paper this sounds almost humorous, but in the soul of a man it is a fire that burns hotly. This is not wrong or bad—it just is. Contrary to some current politically correct male-bashing these days, castration fear is not a sign of immaturity, it is a part of being a male. The sooner we recognize it and begin to open a path for men to celebrate humility, the sooner men can spiritually grow and be more faithful.

> Humble yourselves therefore under the mighty hand of God, that in due time he may exalt you. Cast all your anxieties on him, for he cares about you. Be sober, be watchful.[11]

The following story is of a novice golfer who went out with three other players. On his first tee shot, the ball was sliced badly and ended up in the rough. When the player got to his ball, he found it sitting on top of an anthill. This was no ordinary anthill; it had a population of almost 1,000 ants. When it was his turn, the man looked down, lined up his shoulders and swung. He swung low, and hit the anthill but not his ball, which remained steadfastly on top of the hill. The head of the club had plowed through the ant hill and killed half the population. On his next turn, the golfer took another low swing and again killed half the ant population. This pattern continued until there were just two ants left. As he was lining up to take his swing, one of the ants said to the other, "If we want to live, we'd better get on the ball!"

As Christian men, we need to get on the ball and uncover humility as a God-given grace within our souls. We spend most of our lives as men trying to follow the American myth of rugged individualism, independence, emotionless living, superiority, spiritual blandness, and perfection. We must not forget that Christ's message is to take off this mask of competition and to live in humility. Not as hapless victims or downtrodden whiners, but as strong, obedient, and faithful servants. Indeed, it takes much more courage, strength, vision, and faith to be humble than it ever does to wear a mask of competition.

It is important to note that in every conversion story in Scripture the element of humility is present. To be humble is to no longer be lost, going from door to door seeking a way out. It is to accept our calling to the spiritual disciplines of the faith and to live accordingly.

And when the ten heard it, they became indignant
at James and John. And Jesus called them to him and said to them,
"You know that those who are supposed to rule over the Gentiles lord
it over them, and their great men exercise authority over them.
But it shall not be so among you; but whoever would be great
among you shall be
your servant, and whoever would be first among you must be
slave of all. For the Son of man also came not to
be served but to serve,
and to give his life for many."[12]

DISCUSSION QUESTIONS

1. What did this chapter mean to you?

2. What is it like for you to always have to be competitive? Give examples.

3. What do you do to avoid competition? Give examples.

4. What biblical men do you identify with in your desire to compete?

5. What masks do you wear when you are competing?

6. Describe your experiences of humility.

7. Tell about the joys you know of humility.

8. Which Christian disciplines help you move from competition to humility?

—in an active sense

—in a passive sense

—in a sensual way

—in a spiritual way

9. Which of the seven traditional Christian sins keep you away from living with humility?

10. How are the nine gifts of the Holy Spirit active in the removal of this mask?

Chapter 11

The Mask of Institutional Religion Hides a Man's Desire for Spiritual Growth

While they were going, behold, some of the guards went into the city and told the chief priests all that had taken place. And when they had assembled with the elders and taken counsel, they gave a sum of money to the soldiers and said, "tell people, 'His disciples came by night and stole him away while we were asleep.' And if this comes to the governor's ears, we will satisfy him and keep you out of trouble." So they took the money and did as they were directed; and this story has been spread among the Jews to this day.

—Matthew 28:11-15

One of my favorite activities used to be working out at a local health club in Virginia Beach. The club had a swimming pool, weight rooms, hot tub, sauna, and an indoor track. It was a great place to work on the spiritual discipline of body self-care, prayer, solitude, and community all year long. On the second floor of the facility, in a balcony-type structure, overlooking a large weight room area, was a row of stationary bicycles. There were about twenty bikes in a straight row all along this area. One day I was riding a bike for my one-hour workout. There was nobody else riding a bike near me. After about half an hour, a man came and started riding the bike right next to me. For the entire remaining half hour, I smelled a bad body odor. In fact, I was afraid it was one of those odors that would stay in my nose all day. Obviously this will happen from time to time in a health spa, but it certainly was annoying to be offended for half an hour by someone else's odor. Finally I was done and I went quickly down to the locker room to change for the hot tub. Nobody was in the same aisle of lockers as me that day. While changing I noticed that same awful smell. While going to the hot tub I noticed that same awful smell. I stopped and quietly smelled my own body . . . and discovered that I was the one who carried the odor!

We, as a church, have spent a lot of time pointing out the sins of others. We have spent a lot of time sniffing around in other peoples' and institutions' lives to direct attention to where there is an odor of sin. In the truest sense of confession, however, we must confess that from time to time we as a church carry a bit of an odor as well. A smell we are somewhat loathe to sniff, but nonetheless one that is present. John the Baptist has called us to prepare the way of the Lord, and one way of doing this is to confess our sins, individually and as a church. One confession of the church is that we have fostered for people a strong sense of obligation to the church while downplaying a sense of personal spiritual growth. In particular for men, we have encouraged commitment to the church as an institution, a physical building that needs care, but we have not encouraged personal conversion and transformation of the soul. The result has been that we as men can teach and preach, build and repair, account and govern, but we have souls that are remarkably unaffected by our faith. The mask we hide behind is one of good and decent commitment to the institutional church. This, in and of itself, is not bad. The problem arises when that is the extent of our faith. To be an institutional churchman does not necessarily equate with one who has a strong personal relationship with Jesus Christ and one who is constantly seeking personal spiritual growth. In fact, it is probably quite true that some who are the most active in institutional church-type leadership are still wearing the masks of competition, performance, production and control, and institutional church, which leaves little room for spiritual growth.

This controversy is not new. Jesus constantly had to contend with Jews who were trying to restrict him with law. There was concern for the institutional synagogue over spiritual growth. More concern was shown for dietary law, legal rights, and social customs than for growth in faith. Jesus was well aware of this when he told the parable of the vineyard.[1] The son of the owner, who represented Jesus, was rejected and killed. The owner in the parable, representing God, then killed the tenants. Aware that this message was for them, they tried to arrest Jesus. They were choosing the status quo, the institutional religion, over spiritual growth. Jesus was calling them to freedom from the law, freedom from obligatory faith, and freedom from the institution; but they chose the familiar and shunned spiritual growth. Even at the end, the chief priests and elders did not acknowledge Jesus as the Christ and the liberator. When the tomb was found empty and the truth was made known, they bribed the guards for silence in order to protect the institution. Smell something?

Today, the so-called mainline churches are experiencing an unprecedented decline. There is no denomination that is not downsizing and radically restructuring. Membership nationwide reveals a decline over the past decade, and church attendance wanes. The baby-boomer generation is being blamed for this. Experts say they are just not joiners or people who commit to institutions. Scouting programs, civic groups, PTA associations, and most other mainstays in American culture are experiencing the same phenomenon. The younger people today seem to approach everything with a "What's in this for me?" or "What will I get out of this?" mind-set. Commitment, or sacrifice for the good of the organization, is becoming an ancient term. From boardrooms, to family life, to professional sports, loyalty is also becoming a relic. So, what is the message for the church? Remember the dinosaur, a species that became extinct years ago? Scientists tell us that one reason they became extinct is that some of them could no longer find food. The dinosaur with the long, stiff necks ate all the vegetation they could reach, and because they could not bend their necks to reach more food, they starved to death. The Psalmist and Ezekiel both called the people of their time "stiff-necked," people who could no longer feed themselves of their faith because of their stubbornness. Perhaps the message to us today is that we, too, are causing our own extinction because we have become too stiff-necked in trying to save institutions at the expense of feeding ourselves the nourishment of Christ. We have tried to institutionalize a faith that will not be tamed and organized to death. Clearly the message is before us, to take off masks of institutional religion and experience the work and the joy of spiritual growth through the mercy of Christ and the celebration of the thirteen disciplines.

Men typically like rules and order. We typically like to have things well defined, operations running smoothly, structures clear, no loose ends around, and responsibilities delegated. This is perhaps too much of a generalization, and certainly not true for all men, but it is relatively accurate. Men like institutional structure. We might like to support it, be in it, rebel against it, or criticize it. But, nonetheless, we like it there. It is comfortable to us. It gives us definition on how to perform, produce, compulsively work, and compete against each other and other institutions. An institution is a group to be with to avoid loneliness, a place to control or be controlled, and a socially acceptable place to vent or store up anger. Put men in a room together and very soon we will have officers, meeting times, by-laws, and law enforcers. It is in our very nature! And this is not bad or wrong, it just "is." But Jesus Christ did not call us to comfort or overstructure. He called us to freedom, personal relationship, and loyalty to the cross. The church is the body of Christ on earth, but it is not the body of Christ. Our commitment needs to be to the flesh and blood of our Savior, not the bricks and walls of our churches. So the massive changes in denominations and institutional religion today may be scary, but they may be the very presence of the Holy Spirit calling us again to not be so stiff-necked and legalistic.

The prophet Ezekiel was the first to speak to the people about individual responsibility. He lived in a culture that embraced individual responsibility for the common good. If one person sinned, all were held responsible. Ezekiel's words of individual accountability were a whole new concept to the Hebrews. He wrote:

> Yet you say, "Why should not the son suffer for the iniquity of the father?" When the son has done what is lawful and right, and has been careful to observe all my statutes, he shall surely live. The soul that sins shall die. The son shall not suffer for the iniquity of the father, nor the father suffer for the iniquity of the son; the righteousness of the righteous shall be upon himself, and the wickedness of the wicked shall be upon himself.[2]

Ezekiel declared that every individual was responsible for himself; nobody was to be blamed because of another's actions. This is, in large part, what is being said when we take off the mask of institutional religion and free our God-given desire for spiritual growth. I am responsible for my faith and my relationship with Jesus Christ. I will belong to the church, not to help sustain the institution per se, but for the growth of my faith and what I can offer for the growth of faith in others. The institutional church then becomes a means, not an end, in our spiritual growth. This is a very significant change in the way our institutional churches have operated, but it is the only way to more dynamic and transformational faith. When we do become less stiff-necked and not so worried about church creeds and laws, the Lord will be there to sustain us in growth. Ezekiel presents God's promise of this: "A new heart I will give you, and a new spirit I will put within you and I will take out of your flesh the heart of stone and give you a heart of flesh. And I will put my spirit within you, and cause you to walk in my statutes and be careful to observe my ordinances."[3] This smells refreshing! When we seek spiritual growth and let down the mask of institutional religion, we are intimately inviting Christ into our souls.

For a man, to invite Christ "into" himself, is a potentially frightening thing. We have spent our entire lives keeping others out (emotionally and physically). So, to open up and let Christ in to direct our lives is none too easy a task. We have been trained, taught, rewarded, expected, and perhaps even genetically predispositioned to be in control, independent, and not needy. How can we be expected to know how to make an exception for Christ? This is, in part, why men are not that active in church or regular attendees, it is almost unnatural to worship and bow down before God when we are supposed to take care of ourselves. Biblically speaking, this is blasphemy and today's man is on its borderline when we do not surrender our lives to Christ and seek spiritual growth. Essentially, this means taking so much of the upbringing we have received, along with the cultural messages we have been given, and erasing them. Then, we must replace them with Christ's words for us and a lifestyle involved with the spiritual disciplines given to us in our faith. Remember, we do not earn salvation. The grace of God is an unmerited mercy, but we must also do our part. Our part in removing the mask of institutional religion and seeking Christian spiritual growth, much to the shock and fear of most men, begins with surrender. The seed must be in the soil for the flower to germinate.

In 1980 I was a criminal investigator for the Attorney General of Pennsylvania. I lived alone in an apartment in Harrisburg, Pennsylvania. My work involved many sensitive criminal investigations and a lot of travel. I did not have any close friends at work or in the community, and I did not attend church. My hours off work were spent sleeping, watching TV, going to bars with co-workers, and generally waiting to go back to work. I truly believed in the mission of our work, and I lived for it. One night I was awakened at about 2:00 a.m. by the smell of smoke. Thanks to my fire company training, I was quickly alert to the seriousness of the situation. I felt the bedroom door with the back of my hand and it was hot. It was also beginning to vibrate, which means the fire was intense on the other side of the door, and it was beginning to suck for more oxygen. That meant a very serious danger to me, so I jumped out my bedroom window. The entire apartment was gutted by fire and smoke, and I lost everything I owned, save a few slightly charred items (including my Bible and Confirmation book from the Presbyterian Church). That early morning, sitting on the lawn, alone after the fire department and neighbors had left, I experienced a sadness and loneliness I had never known before. I was startled with how empty my life was, how I lacked commitment to God and any person, how cavalier I had been about existence, and how, if I had died, only my family would have missed me.

I did not know it at the time, but that was a very convicting conversion experience for me. My work and my lifestyle were suddenly exposed to me as quite shallow and selfish. I also learned that I could not always take care of myself or be in control; sometimes things were beyond my ability. As I read the eight masks in this book I must laugh a bit, because I was wearing them all for so many years, and usually with such pride. Give me a task and I would perform with gusto. I had no pain or hurt (I thought) because I could channel my anger to criminals and the justice system. I had a gun, and I was in control. I compulsively ate and drank beer, but because I also compulsively exercised, it was not obvious. I loved to produce work because I was always awarded with more work! I did not know I was lonely because I had no close friends and expected none. I did not attend church, so institutional religion was something I avoided. In September 1991 I entered seminary at Duke University to get some answers for my life. I did not know I was worn down and tired from wearing all these masks, but I did know "something" was wrong. Somehow, thank God, my family, church, and Christ had planted a seed earlier in my life for my faith to now begin growing. It took the heat of a fire to begin the process, but most seeds need some heat to open.

I did not feel called in the traditional sense to "be a minister in a church," but to learn more about the Christian faith. Perhaps this is, in part, why spiritual growth and not institutional church means more to me. Having almost lost my life in the fire, I am aware salvation is in faith, not structure. The church is necessary, but only as a vehicle to help us along the road of Christian spiritual growth. I did begin local church ministry upon graduation because it seemed like an excellent opportunity to continue spiritual growth with others and to serve an institution that helped save my life. Like so many of my peers, I am truly overjoyed with the parish ministry, but also a bit saddened. Too much of what we have to do involves keeping the institution alive and not enough involves spiritual-growth endeavors. I see people fall away from the church because their spiritual needs are not being met. I feel drained sometimes because my own spiritual needs are not met. Yet, as I preach and know, and as Ezekiel wrote, we are each responsible for ourselves. I must find ways to maintain good spiritual discipline, and so must others who seek to grow. The letter to the church in Thessalonica seems to best state how to do this:

Rejoice always,
pray constantly, give thanks in all circumstances;
for this is the will of God in Jesus Christ for you.
Do not quench the Spirit, do not despise prophesying,
but test everything; hold fast what is good,
abstain from every form of evil.[4]

DISCUSSION QUESTIONS

1. What did this chapter mean to you?

2. What is it like for you to be a part of the institutional church? Give examples.

3. What do you avoid about the institutional church? Give examples.

4. What biblical men do you identify with in the institutional church?

5. What masks do you wear in the institutional church?

6. Describe your experiences of spiritual growth.

7. Tell about the joys you know of spiritual growth.

8. Which Christian disciplines help you move from institutional religion to spiritual growth?

   —in an active sense

   —in a passive sense

—in a sensual way

—in a spiritual way

9. Which of the seven traditional Christian sins keep you away from spiritual growth?

10. How are the nine gifts of the Holy Spirit active in the removal of this mask?

Chapter 12

Conclusion and Suggestions

I was recently at a luncheon at Richmond International Raceway where NASCAR race car driver Jeff Gordon spoke. Someone asked him how in the world, he as a relative newcomer to the Winston Cup circuit, could drive so well in the midst of some thirty other cars at speeds near 190 mph. His answer was very brief: "I focus only on driving my own car." This, in large part, is the essence of spiritual growth. We must concentrate on our own souls. Even in the midst of hectic schedules, busy days, and others racing all around us, we must stay focused on our own souls.

After the fire, but particularly after my surgical experience and near-death battle, I know that if I do not care for myself, with God's help, no one else will. I say this out of a sense of confession, not loneliness. Ultimately, it is not our parents' responsibility, our wives' responsibility, our pastors' responsibility—it is our own responsibility to nurture our souls, with God's grace. Just as Jeff Gordon is a relative novice on the Winston Cup circuit, we may be relative newcomers to the racetrack of spiritual growth. When we focus on our souls, this is the best we can do.

- I will testify to you that friendship is beneath the mask of control.
- I will testify to you that solitude and community are beneath the mask of loneliness.
- I will testify to you that "being" is beneath the mask of producing.
- I will testify to you that pain and hurt are beneath the mask of anger and rage.
- I will testify to you that humility is beneath the mask of competition.
- I will testify to you that love is beneath the mask of compulsive living.

- I will testify to you that acceptance is beneath the mask of performing.
- I will testify to you that spiritual growth is beneath the mask of institutional religion.

Worship, prayer, surrender, body care and exercise, service, solitude, friendship, human sexuality, financial commitment, simplicity, confession/forgiveness, community, and fasting are the historic avenues for Christians to seek spiritual growth. In my life, I have found the love, goodness, peace, joy, kindness, faithfulness, patience, gentleness, and self-control in and around these disciplines. I am also regularly tempted by the sins of anger, envy, greed, gluttony, laziness, lust, and pride. By the grace of God, which cannot be emphasized enough, we can do battle with evil and transform our lives. By the grace of God, men need no longer get too comfortable with, or hide behind, so many masks. By the grace of God, we can slowly remove masks we have been wearing for too many years, and reveal to ourselves, to God, and the world, our true selves as created by God.

But as to the times and seasons, brethren, you have no need
to have anything written to you. For you yourselves knew
well that the day of the Lord will come like a thief in the night.
When people say "There is peace and security," then
sudden destruction will come upon them as travail comes upon
a woman with child, and there will be no escape.
But you are not in darkness, brethren,
for that day to surprise you like a thief.
For you are all sons of light and sons of the day; we are not
of the night and of darkness.
So then let us not sleep, as others do, but let us keep awake and sober.
For those who sleep, sleep at night, and those who get drunk
get drunk at night. But, since we belong to the day, let us be
sober, and put on the breastplate of faith and love, and
for a helmet the hope of salvation. For God has not destined us for
wrath, but to obtain salvation through our Lord Jesus Christ,
who died for us that whether we wake or sleep
we might live with him. Therefore,
encourage one another and build one another up
just as you are doing.[1]

REGISTRATION FORM

1. Name: _____

2. Address: _____

_____

3. Telephone/fax: _____

4. Prior men's work or spirituality work: _____

_____

5. What is your goal in participating in this group?:_____

_____

6. What is your image of a man?: _____

_____

7. What is missing in your life?: _____

_____

8. Name particular biblical men you admire: _____

_____

9. How are your relationships with other men?: _____

_____

10. How is your relationship with Jesus Christ?: _____

_____

MEETING EVALUATION

This form is to be used after each meeting to help guide the leader(s).

1. My goal for tonight was _____

_____

2. My goal was met or not met and _____

_____

3. What was the most helpful tonight? _____

_____

4. What was the least helpful tonight? _____

_____

5. How are you feeling after this session? _____

_____

6. What particular spiritual gift has been opened to you today?

_____

7. What biblical story is most relevant to you after this meeting?

_____

8. Identify what you hope to get out of the next meeting. _____

_____

THE COVENANT OF CONDUCT

This is to be read aloud and agreed upon by every man in the group in the first meeting.

1. I will speak only the truth as I know it.

2. I will honor my own feelings and my spiritual journey, and those of the other men.

3. I will offer respect and Christian friendship to every man here.

4. I will not consume alcohol or any drug prior to, during, or after the meetings.

5. All relationships here are nonviolent and nonsexual.

6. Healing touch is encouraged when appropriate.

7. I will tell no one what is said or occurs here without the expressed consent of all members.

8. I am a Christian man and will strive to uphold the teachings of Jesus Christ.

9. I will offer myself as a healer to any man in the group.

10. If I feel like quitting the group, I will first discuss my feelings and reasons with the group.

OPENING AND CLOSING LITURGY

This is to be used each night to open the meeting.

Be sure to use this liturgy or one the group agrees upon each week. It is essential that you center yourselves and state the purpose for your meeting each time.

Man: My name is_____

Group: Amen. Welcome_____

Man: Tonight I am feeling _____

Man: My moment(s) closest to Christ this week _____

_____

Man: A moment(s) I felt distant from Christ this week _____

_____

Group: Amen, _____. Welcome to this sacred gathering of men.

After each man has gone through this liturgy, which may be brief or could take quite a while, unite in prayer.

Group: Silent prayer

Prayers of petition

Lord's Prayer

CLOSING—any last comments from the men, then a group time of prayer, then dismissal.

CLOSING LITURGY FOR SESSION 9: MASCULINE SPIRITUALITY PROGRAM— RITE OF CHRISTIAN HEALING

Call to Worship

Leader: May the mercy of Christ surround you throughout this season of worship.

Men: May the light of Christ illumine our way to emotional and spiritual healing.

Leader: To receive healing, we must first confess our woundedness.

Men: We confess our wounds and brokenness, we confess our need for Christ's mercy.

Prayer of Centering (St. Ignatius of Loyola)

Unison: Soul of Christ, sanctify me. Body of Christ, save me. Blood of Christ, fill me with life. Water from the side of Christ, wash me. Passion of Christ, strengthen me. O good Jesus, hear me. Within your wounds, conceal me. Allow me not to be separated from you. From the evil foe defend me. At the hour of my death call me, And bid me come to you, That with your saints I may praise you. For ever and ever. Amen.

Collect

Unison: God of ancient wisdom and emerging truth, Creator of the universe, we proclaim our trust and faith in you. We join now in this ritual of healing as men, sacred and beautiful, together seeking spiritual growth. We admit our woundedness, we embrace your holy forgiveness, we desire to be united with you, and we seek to sincerely follow your commands. Transform us, Lord Christ, not to the standards of this world, but to the pilgrim's journey of Christian truth. In Jesus name. Amen.

Hymn of Praise

Proclamations of the Men

This is a time for each man to speak to the group, to offer final words after the formal nine-week program.

Presence of Sacred Light

Now the leader should light the Christ candle and place it before the men.

Each man should come forward and light his candle from the Christ candle.

Preparation of the Elements

The leader should offer a prayer of blessing over the oil, water, and ash.

Rite of Christian Healing

Each man should come forward now, before the leader, to receive the sign of the cross on both his palms with the ointment made of oil, water, and ash.

Man: My name is ——————. I confess Jesus Christ as my
Lord and Savior.

Leader: —————— , Jesus Christ is your Lord and Savior.

Group: —————— , may Jesus Christ bless you forever.
Amen.

Hymn of Consecration

Prayers of the Community of Men

Benediction and Blessing

Dismissal

Appendix

Biblical References
for Masculine Spiritual Growth

The following chapter is for your use in looking at various men and circumstances in the Bible that relate to masculine spiritual growth. These men struggled with many of the same personal and spiritual issues with which we struggle today. We can learn from them, laugh with them, cry with them, grow with them, repent with them; in short, we can celebrate life with them. It is important for the Christian man to know his journey is not unique; he joins a host of fellow pilgrims along the way. These men are our brothers, broken and blessed by God, just like us. Take time, take plenty of time, to read these biblical accounts and let the spiritual richness of these sacred men and these events grow in your soul. This is a partial list of men and men's issues from Scripture.

Fathers and Sons

Scripture	Account Summary	General Theme
Genesis 2:24	. . . man leaves father and mother	isolation/separation
Genesis 12:1-8	God calls Abraham to leave home	journey of unknowing
Genesis 17:1-10	God's covenant with Abraham	responsibility
Genesis 16:1-16 and Genesis 21:1-21	Abraham, Sarah, Hagar, Isaac, Ishmael	rejection, envy, betrayal and reconciliation
Genesis 49:1-28	Jacob blesses his twelve sons	father's blessing
I Samuel 2:1-26	Eli's irresponsible sons	fathering sons
I Samuel 14:24-30	Saul failed Jonathan	deceit
II Samuel 16:22	Absalom follows the father he hated	heredity
II Samuel 18:33	David grieves Absalom's death	father's remorse and grief
Ezekiel 18:19-20	son's sins are not the father's sins	responsibility
Matthew 1:1-17	genealogy of Jesus Christ	family ties
Matthew 1:18-25	Joseph follows God's word	obedience
Matthew 1:19-20	James and John depart	call of discipleship
Matthew 3:17	"Thou art my beloved Son. . ."	father's blessing
Luke 15: 11-32	story of father and two sons	envy, repentance, forgiveness

Mothers and Sons

Scripture	Account Summary	General Theme
Genesis 16:1-16 and Genesis 21:1-16	Sarah-Isaac; Hagar-Ishmael	betrayal and abandonment
Genesis 25: 19-28	Rebekah, Jacob, and Esau	manipulation, favoritism
Judges 13:6-7, 24	Samson the Nazarite	pledge of sacrifice to Lord
I Samuel 1:1-28	birth of Samuel to Hannah	perseverence, gift receiving
Luke 2:1-40	Mary's sacrifice for Jesus	mother's faith
John 2:1-11	Jesus' mother is rebuked	boundary of son
John 19:26-27	"Woman, behold your son . . ."	separation

Men Seek Help

Scripture	Account Summary	General Theme
Exodus 4:10-17	". . .I can't . . ."	Moses asks God for help
Joshua 10:12-14	Joshua asks God to still sun	asking God for help
Judges 6:15	Gideon admits vulnerability	needs assistance
I Samuel 17:39	I'll go as I am	help from within self
I Kings 17:8-16	Elijah sustained by the widow	I need . . .
II Kings 4:18-20	father sends injured son to wife	I need your help
Psalm 23	the Lord is my shepherd	I need him
Psalm 116	delivered my soul from death	I need saving
Jeremiah 17:14-18	heal me, O Lord	I need the Lord's aid
Ezekiel 3:3-4	prophet eats the scroll	witness seeking saving
Matthew 9:23	healing of Jairus's daughter	to save child
Matthew 8:5-13	centurian asks Jesus to heal servant	for healing of another
Mark 10:46-52	blind Bartimaeus asks for healing	physical healing
Luke 5:12-16	leper is healed	physical healing
Luke 11:1	Lord, teach us to pray	spiritual activity
John 3:1-21	Nicodemus comes to Jesus	faithfulness
John 14:8	Lord, show us the father	signs for belief
Acts 5:34	Gamaliel speaks to people	wisdom
Acts 8:26-40	Ethiopian seeks Philip's help	spiritual knowledge
Acts 15:36-41	Paul/Silas depart Mark/Barnabas	disagreement
Philippians 2:1-11	any incentive, any participation . . .	companionship
Philemon 8-18	Paul hopes to help Onesimus	friendship, forgiveness

Mens' Relationships with Other Men

Scripture	Account Summary	General Theme
Exodus 4:18	Moses returns to help Israelites	commitment, fellowship
Deuteronomy 34:9b	Moses laid hands on Joshua	mentor blessing
Joshua 6:1-27	together the people seize Jericho	unity

Scripture	Account Summary	General Theme
Joshua 7:6-26	Achan's betrayal causes suffering	betrayal
Judges 15:1-3	Samson's wife given by father	betrayal
I Samuel 20:1-42	David and Jonathan	friendship, love
II Samuel 12:1-25	Nathan convicts David	rebuke, accountability
Proverbs 27:17	. . . one man sharpens another . . .	community, brotherhood
I Kings 21:1-29	Ahab steals Naboth's vineyard	theft, betrayal
II Kings 4:8-37	Elisha revives the boy	mentoring, salvation
II Kings 2:23-25	Elisha curses boys	rage and anger
II Kings 5:1-27	curing of Naaman through Elisha	humility
Jonah 4:1-5	desire that others suffer	reluctance, repentance
Malachi 3:1-4	Lord's messenger	repentance
Matthew 3:1-12	calling to repentance by John	faithfulness despite risk
Matthew 26:6-13	Jesus at home of leper	acceptance
Luke 5:17-21	friends lower friend through window	love, healing
Luke 9:23-27	save life, lose life	discipleship
John 6:5-6	Jesus tests Philip with question	a test
John 18:12-14	Caiaphas sits in power	judgment
Acts 9:10-17	Ananias helps Paul	salvation, healing
Acts 9:32-34	Peter heals Aeneas	healing
Acts 23:12-22	Jews plot to kill Paul	conspiracy bond
I John 2:7-11	brethren to love one another	love, friendship, community

Man's Experience of God's Presence

Scripture	Account Summary	General Theme
Genesis 9:1-19	God's covenant with Noah	promise, love, presence
Genesis 28:10-17	Jacob's dream at Bethel	presence, blessing
Genesis 32:22-32	Jacob wrestles with angel	transformation
Exodus 3:1-15	blessing, hope, and naming (I am)	call
Exodus 19:16-25	God meets Moses at Sinai	decalogue, commitment
Isaiah 6:1-9	here am I, send me	vision, dedication
Jeremiah 1:5	consecrated in your mother's womb	creation blessing
II Chronicles 1:1-17	Solomon asks for wisdom	gift of wisdom
Matthew 1:18-25	birth of Jesus	God's incarnation
Matthew 5:1-20	Beatitudes	new life
Matthew 16:13-20	Peter names Jesus as the Christ	confession, commitment
Luke 1:5-2:40	angels, birth of John and Jesus	announcements, new life
Luke 17:11-19	ten lepers cleansed	cleansing, thanksgiving
John 9:1-8	healing of man born blind	healing, renewal
Acts 8:26	angel directs Philip	spiritual direction
Acts 9:1-22	Saul converted to the faith	conversion, companionship
Acts 10:1-48	conversion of Cornelius	terror, faith
I Corinthians 3:16	body is temple of Lord	body theology

Humanity of Man

Scripture	Account Summary	General Theme
Exodus 2:11-14	Moses kills Egyptian and flees	rage, denial, fear, murder
Exodus 17:3	people rebel against Moses	rebellion, greed, lust
I Samuel 3:1-11	call of Samuel, who goes to Eli	spiritual confusion
I Samuel 18:28	Saul envies David	envy
I Samuel 24:8-15	David spares Saul's life	compassion, forgiveness
II Samuel 1:1-27	David grieves over Saul and Jonathan	sadness, grief, loss
II Samuel 11:1-27	David betrays Uriah and Bathsheba	betrayal, lust, deceit, rage
I Kings 19:1-8	Elijah fears Jezebel and flees	fear, uncertainty, loss
II Kings 5:20-27	Gehazi lies to Elisha	deceit, greed, lying
Job 3:1	cursing day of birth	spiritual anxiety
Matthew 2:1-23	Herod the Great seeks to kill Jesus	jealousy, fear, gluttony
Matthew 2:16	Herod the Great murders males	murder, rage, greed, anger
Matthew 14:10-11	Judas seeks to betray Jesus	betrayal, greed, power
Matthew 20:20-28	James and John seek honor	pride, selfishness
Matthew 22:36-40	Great Commandment	love, community, friendship
Luke 10:29-37	Good Samaritan parable	community, kindness
Luke 11:1-13	cannot serve God and mammon	dishonesty, selfishness
Luke 23:18-25	Barabbas chosen over Jesus	fear, confusion
John 12:9-11	conspiracy to kill enemy	envy, pride
John 18:15-27	Peter's denial of Jesus	betrayal, lying
Acts 6:1-8	Stephen's call and ministry	evangelism, faith, commitment
Acts 8:14-24	Simon tries to buy Holy Spirit	greed, spiritual ignorance
Acts 17:16-34	Paul at Athens	commitment, strength
Romans 9:1-5	Paul sad at Israel's unbelief	sadness, grief, love
Philippians 1:3-11	Paul's words of thanks	thanksgiving, praise

Reference Notes

Chapter 1

1. James Nelson. *Body Theology.* (Louisville, KY: Westminster/John Knox Press, 1992), pp. 42-43.
2. Psalm 116:5-7.
3. Exodus 3:7-12.
4. Joshua 9:14-15.
5. Kenneth Solomon and Norman Levy (eds.). *Men in Transition.* (New York: Plenum Press, 1982), pp. 58-59.
6. James Hollis. *Under Saturn's Shadow: The Wounding and Healing of Men.* (Toronto, Canada: Inner City Books, 1994), p. 11.

Chapter 2

1. Patrick M. Arnold. *Wildmen, Warriors and Kings.* (New York: Crossroads Publishing, 1991), p. 7.
2. John 13:34-35.
3. Sam Keen *Fire in the Belly.* (New York: Bantam Books, 1991), p. 5.
4. Ibid., p. 175.
5. E. Brooks Holifield *A History of Pastoral Care in America.* (Nashville, TN: Abingdon, 1983), p. 330.
6. Arnold, p. 14.
7. Aaron Kipnis. *Knights Without Armor.* (Los Angeles, CA: Jeremy Tarcher, Inc., 1991), pp. 25-27.
8. Ibid., 9.
9. Tom Owen-Towle. *Brother-Spirit.* (San Diego, CA: Bald Eagle Mountain Press, 1991), p. 38.
10. Arnold, 3.
11. Acts 2: 1-21.
12. Tilden Edwards. *Spiritual Friend.* (New York: Paulist Press, 1980), p. 180-182.
13. Ibid., pp. 189-191.

Chapter 3

1. Matthew 16:25.
2. *The Collected Works of Saint John of the Cross*, translated by Kieran Kavanaugh, OCD and Otilio Rodriguez, OCD. (ICS Publications, Washington Province of Discalced Carmelite Friars Inc., Washington, DC, 1991), p. 18.

3. Ibid., page 19.

4. Psalm 119:61.

5. Psalm 118:12.

6. *The Collected Works of St. John of the Cross*, translated by Kieran Kavanaugh, OCD and Otilio Rodriguez, (ICS Publications, Washington Province of Discalced Carmelite Friars, Inc.: Washington, DC, 1991), p. 155.

7. Ibid., pp. 164-165.

8. Isaiah 26:17-18.

9. Hebrews 12:11.

10. Exodus 20:3.

11. Matthew 4:10.

12. Thomas Merton, *No Man Is an Island.* (New York: New Directions Publishing, 1983), p. 230.

13. Romans 7:14-23.

14. Matthew 6:9-13, John 15:7.

15. Mark 1:35, Mark 14:32-42, Luke 22:42.

16. John 17:20-26.

17. Luke 11:1.

18. I Thessalonians 5:17.

19. Henri Nouwen, *Reaching Out.* (New York: Doubleday, 1966), p. 135.

20. Yushi Nomura, *Desert Wisdom.* (Garden City, NJ: Doubleday and Company, 1982), p. 22.

21. Matthew 20:25-28.

22. Nouwen, *Reaching Out*, 39.

23. Matthew 4:1-11, 14:13, 14:23, 17:1-9, 26:36-46, Luke 6:12.

24. Luke 12:34.

25. Luke 12:15-21.

26. I Corinthians 3:16.

27. I Corinthians 6:19.

28. James B. Nelson, *Body Theology.* (Westminster/John Knox Press: Louisville, KY, 1992), p. 9.

29. James B. Nelson, *The Intimate Connection.* (Philadelphia, PA: The Westminster Press, 1988), p. 23.

30. Song of Solomon 4:8-15.

31. II Samuel 12:21, Matthew 4:2, Mark 2:18.

32. Joel 2:13.

33. Leviticus 23:27.

34. Luke 18:12.

35. Richard J. Foster, *Celebration of Discipline.* (San Francisco, CA: Harper and Row, 1988), p. 51.

36. Matthew 6:16, 9:15.

37. Mark 8:34.

38. Matthew 10:39.

39. St. Ignatius of Loyola, *The Spiritual Exercises*, translated by Elizabeth Meier Tetlow (Lanham, MD: University Press of America, 1987), p. 11.

40. Philippians 2:4-7.
41. I Timothy 2:5.
42. John 20:23.
43. I John 1:9.
44. Luke 9:3-4.
45. Luke 10:3-4.
46. Romans 14:7-8.
47. Matthew 19:16-22.
48. Luke 12:33.
49. Proverbs 27:17.
50. I Samuel 18:1.
51. Matthew 28:16-20.

Chapter 4

1. Henri Nouwen, *Reaching Out.* (New York: Doubleday, 1975) pp. 26-27.
2. Anonymous letter from a man.
3. Anonymous letter from a man.
4. Philip Leroy Culbertson, *New Adam: The Future of Masculine Spirituality.* (Minnesota: Augsburg Fortress, 1992), pp. 11-12.
5. Michael Cox, *Handbook of Christian Spirituality.* (New York: The Aquarian Press, 1985), p. 114.
6. Matthew 10:39.

Chapter 5

1. II Kings 2:19-22.
2. II Kings 4:1-7.
3. II Kings 4:8-37.
4. II Kings 4:38-44.
5. II Kings 5:1-27.
6. Luke 8:40-56.
7. Jeremiah 8:18-9:1.
8. Jeremiah 31:9a.
9. Lamentations 3:49-59.

Chapter 6

1. Exodus 32:1-35.
2. II Samuel 11:1-27.
3. II Samuel 13:1-39.
4. Luke 15:11-32.
5. Acts 5:1-11.
6. Galatians 5:16.

7. Genesis 50:21.
8. Psalms 130:5.
9. Jeremiah 31:33d.
10. I Corinthians 13:1-13.
11. Philemon 16.

Chapter 7

1. I Samuel 17:38-39.
2. Romans 10:8-13.

Chapter 8

1. Genesis 37:1-36.
2. Exodus 7:8-11:10.
3. I Kings 21:1-29.
4. II Kings 5:20-27.
5. Matthew 26:69-75.
6. Acts 7:54-60.
7. I Corinthians 1:22-25.
8. Proverbs 27:17.
9. Acts 8:26-40.
10. I Samuel 18:1.
11. I Samuel 20:41b-42.

Chapter 9

1. Exodus 3:4c.
2. II Kings 5:10b.
3. Isaiah 40:1-2.
4. Luke 18:14.
5. Ephesians 2:4-10.
6. Hebrews 13:5b.
7. I Samuel 3:1-10.
8. Genesis 32:28a.
9. Exodus 3:4c.
10. Joshua 1:2.
11. Job 42:2-4.
12. Psalms 51:1-2, 6-9.
13. Psalms 116:7.
14. Matthew 6:25-27.
15. Romans 10:8b-10.
16. Psalm 23.

Chapter 10

1. Matthew 20:20-28.
2. Genesis 4:1-26.
3. Genesis 27:1-45.
4. Matthew 20:1-16.
5. Acts 8:14-24.
6. Romans 14:10.
7. Genesis 32:22-32.
8. Exodus 4:10-17.
9. Judges 6:15.
10. Matthew 23:11-12.
11. I Peter 5:6-7.
12. Mark 10:41-45.

Chapter 11

1. Mark 12:1-12.
2. Ezekiel 18:19-20.
3. Ezekiel 36:26-27.
4. I Thessalonians 5:16-22.

Chapter 12

1. I Thessalonians 5:1-11.

Bibliography

Abrams, Jeremiah (ed.). *Reclaiming the Inner Child*. Los Angeles: Tarcher Publishing, 1990.

Anonymous. *Hope and Recovery: 12-Step Healing for Compulsive Sexual Behavior*. Minneapolis, MN: Compcare, 1987.

Arnold, Patrick M. *Wildmen, Warriors, and Kings*. New York: Crossroads Publishing, 1991.

Bly, Robert. *Iron John: A Book About Men*. New York: Addison-Wesley Publishing Company, 1990.

Bolen, Jean Shinoda. *Gods in Everyman*. New York: Harper and Row Publishing, 1989.

Bonhoeffer, Dietrich. *Life Together*. New York: Harper and Row Publishing, 1954.

Bowers, Margaretta. *Conflicts in the Clergy*. New York: Thomas Nelson and Sons, 1963.

Bradshaw, John. *The Family*. Deerfield Beach, FL: Health Communication, Inc., 1988.

Brother Roger of Taize. *Awakened from Within*. New York: Doubleday, 1987.

Browning, Robert (ed.). *The Pastor As Religious Educator*. Birmingham, AL: Religious Education Press, 1989.

Capps, Donald. *Life Cycle Theory and Pastoral Care*. Philadelphia: Fortress Press, 1983.

Carmody, John. *Toward a Male Spirituality*. Mystic, CT: Twenty-Third Publications, 1988.

Christ, Carol P. and Judith Plaskow. *Womanspirit Rising*. San Francisco: Harper and Row, 1979.

Clinebell, Howard J., Jr. *Basic Types of Pastoral Counseling*. Nashville, TN: Abingdon, 1966.

Cox, Michael. *Handbook of Christian Spirituality*. New York: Harper and Row, 1983.

Culbertson, Philip. *New Adam: The Future of Male Spirituality*. Minneapolis, MN: Fortress Press, 1992.

Dayringer, Richard. *The Heart of Pastoral Counseling* (rev. ed.). Binghamton, NY: The Haworth Pastoral Press, 1998.

Edwards, Tilden. *Spiritual Friend*. New York: Paulist Press, 1980.

Erikson, Erik H. *Childhood and Society*. New York: W.W. Norton and Company, 1950.

_____. *Identity and the Life Cycle*. New York: W.W. Norton and Company, 1980.

Evslin, Bernard. *Hermes, Gods and Monsters of the Greek Myths*. New York: Bantam Books, 1966.

Fast, Irene. *Gender Identity*. Hillsdale, NJ: The Analytic Press, 1984.

Foltz, Nancy T. (ed.). *Religious Education in the Small Member Church*. Birmingham, AL: Religious Education Press, 1990.

Fossum, Merle. *Catching Fire: Men Coming Alive in Recovery*. San Francisco: Harper/Hazelden Book, 1989.

Foster, Richard J. *Celebration of Discipline*. San Francisco: Harper and Row, 1988.

Fowler, James W. *Faith Development and Pastoral Care*. Philadelphia: Fortress Press, 1987.

Franklin, Clyde W. III. *The Changing Definition of Masculinity*. New York: Plenum Press, 1984.

Freud, Sigmund. *Outline of Psycho-Analysis*, translated by James Strachey. New York: W.W. Norton, Co., 1949.

Gilligan, Carol. *In a Different Voice*. Cambridge, MA: Harvard University Press, 1982.

Gorman, Margaret (ed.). *Psychology and Religion*. New York: Paulist Press, 1985.

Group for the Advancement of Psychiatry. *The Process of Child Therapy*. New York: Brunner/Mazel Publishers, 1992.

Hamilton, Gregory N. *Self and Others, Object Relations Theory in Practice*. Northvale, NJ: Jason Aronson, Inc., 1988.

Hannah, Barbara. *Jung, His Life and Work*. Boston: Shambhala Publications, 1976.

Harris, Maria. *Dance of the Spirit: The Seven Steps of Women's Spirituality*. New York: Bantam Books, 1978.

————. *Fashion Me a People*. Louisville, KY: Westminster/John Knox Press, 1989.

Hergenhahn, B.R. *An Introduction to Theories of Personality*. Englewood Cliffs, NJ: Prentice-Hall, 1980.

Holifield, E. Brooks. *A History of Pastoral Care in America*. Nashville, TN: Abingdon Press, 1983.

Hollis, James. *Under Saturn's Shadow: The Wounding and Healing of Men*. Toronto, Canada: Inner City Books, 1994.

Jackson, Graham. *The Secret Lore of Gardening: Partners of Male Intimacy*. Toronto, Canada: Inner City Books, 1991.

Jones, Alan. *Exploring Spiritual Direction*. Minneapolis, MN: Winston Press, 1982.

Jung, Carl G. *Symbols of Transformation*. Princeton, NJ: Princeton University Press, 1956.

————. *Man and His Symbols*. New York: Dell Publishing, 1964.

————. *Memories, Dreams and Reflections*. New York: Pantheon Books, 1973.

————. *Aspects of the Masculine*. Princeton, NJ: Princeton University Press, translation by R.F.C. Hull, 1989.

Kauth, Bill. *Men's Friends*. Milwaukee, WI: Human Development Associates, 1991.

Keen, Sam. *Fire in the Belly: On Being a Man.* New York: Bantam Books, 1991.
————. *The Passionate Life.* New York: HarperCollins, 1992.
Kegan, Robert. *The Evolving Self.* Cambridge, MA: Harvard University Press, 1982.
Kelsey, Morton T. *Companions on the Inner Way.* New York: Crossroads Publishing, Inc., 1989.
Kipnis, Aaron R. *Knights Without Armor: A Practical Guide for Men in Quest of the Masculine Soul.* Los Angeles: Jeremy Tarcher, Inc., 1991.
Lee, John. *Flying Boy Book II: The Journey Continues.* Deerfield Beach, FL: Health Communications, 1990.
Lew, Mike. *Victims No Longer: Men Recovering from Incest and Other Sexual Child Abuse.* New York: Nevraumont Publishing Co., 1988.
Liebman, Wayne. *Tending the Fire: Ritual Men's Group.* St. Paul, MN: Ally Press, 1991.
St. Ignatius of Loyola. *The Spiritual Exercises of St. Ignatius of Loyola.* Maryland: The University Press, translated by Elisabeth Meier Tetlow, 1987.
Merton, Thomas. *New Seeds of Contemplation.* New York: New Directions Publishing, 1961.
————. *Contemplative Prayer.* New York: Doubleday, 1969.
————. *No Man Is an Island.* New York: Harcourt Brace Jovanovich, 1983.
Monick, Eugene. *Phallos.* Toronto: Inner City Books, 1990.
————. *Castration and Male Rage.* Toronto: Inner City Books, 1991.
Moore, Robert L. (ed.). *Carl Jung and Christian Spirituality.* New York: Paulist Press, 1988.
Moore, Robert and Douglas Gillette. *King, Warrior, Magician, Lover.* San Francisco: Harper and Row, 1991.
Moore, Thomas. *Care of the Soul.* New York: HarperCollins Publishers, Inc., 1992.
Nelson, James B. *Embodiment: An Approach to Sexuality and Christian Theology.* Minneapolis, MN: Augsburg Fortress Press, 1978.
————. *Intimate Connection: Male Sexuality, Masculine Spirituality.* Philadelphia: The Westminster Press, 1988.
Nicolosi, Joseph. *Reparative Therapy of Male Homosexuality.* Northvale, NJ: Jason Aronson Publishing, 1991.
Nomura, Yushi. *Desert Wisdom.* Garden City, NJ: Doubleday and Company, 1982.
Nouwen, Henri. *Reaching Out.* New York: Doubleday, 1966.
————. *The Wounded Healer.* Garden City, NJ: Image Books, 1979.
————. *The Way of the Heart.* San Francisco: Paulist Press, 1981.
Osherson, Samuel. *Finding Our Fathers.* New York: Fawcett Columbine, 1986.
Owen-Towle, Tom. *Brother Spirit.* San Diego: Bald Eagle Mountain Press, 1991.
Peck, M. Scott. *People of the Lie.* New York: Simon and Schuster, 1983.
Peck, M. Scott. *The Road Less Traveled.* New York: Simon and Schuster, 1978.
Pederson, Loren E. *Dark Hearts: The Unconscious Forces That Shape Men's Lives.* Boston: Shambhala, 1991.

————. *Sixteen Men: Understanding Masculine Personality Types*. Boston: Shambhala, 1993.

Rahner, Karl. *The Practice of Faith*. New York: Crossroad Publishing, 1984.

Rickman, John (ed.). *General Selections from the Work of Sigmund Freud*. New York: Anchor Books, 1957.

Roth, Geneen. *When Food Is Love*. New York: Penguin Books, 1991.

Schaef, Anne Wilson. *Women's Reality*. San Francisco: Harper and Row, 1981.

Seymour, Jack L. and Donald E. Miller (eds.). *Theological Approaches to Christian Education*. Nashville, TN: Abingdon Press, 1990.

Simonton, O. Carl. *Healing Journey*. New York: Bantam Books, 1992.

Smith, D. Moody and Robert A. Spivey. *Anatomy of the New Testament*. New York: Macmillan Publishing Co., 1974.

Stookey, Lawrence Hull. *Baptism: Christ's Act in the Church*. Nashville, TN: Abingdon Press, 1982.

St. John of the Cross. *Collected Works*. Washington, DC: Institute of Carmelite Studies, translated by Kieran Kavanaugh and Otilio Rodriguez, 1991.

Streiker, Lowell D. *Fathering*. Nashville, TN: Abingdon Press, 1989.

Thomas, T. *Men Surviving Incest*. Walnut Creek, CA: Launch Press, 1989.

Thompson, Keith. *To Be a Man*. Los Angeles: Jeremy P. Tarcher, Inc., 1991.

Vanderwall, Francis W. *Spiritual Direction*. New York: Paulist Press, 1981.

Westerhoff, John and O.C. Edwards (eds.). *A Faithful Church, Issues in the History of Cathechesis*. Ridgefield, CT: Morehouse-Barlow Co., 1981.

White, James F. *Christian Worship*. Nashville, TN: Abingdon Press, 1981.

Whitfield, Charles L. *Healing the Child Within*. Deerfield Beach, FL: Health Communications, Inc., 1990.

Willimon, William H. *Worship As Pastoral Care*. Nashville, TN: Abingdon, 1979.

Wise, Carroll. *Pastoral Psychotherapy*. Northvale, NJ: Jason Aronson, Inc., 1983.

Wyly, James. *The Phallic Quest: Priapus and Masculine Inflation*. Toronto, Canada: Inner City Books, 1989.

Index

Order Your Own Copy of
This Important Book for Your Personal Library!

THE EIGHT MASKS OF MEN

A Practical Guide in Spiritual Growth for Men of the Christian Faith

_____ in hardbound at $39.95 (ISBN: 0-7890-0415-1)

_____ in softbound at $19.95 (ISBN: 0-7890-0416-X)

COST OF BOOKS_____

OUTSIDE USA/CANADA/
MEXICO: ADD 20%_____

POSTAGE & HANDLING_____
(US: $3.00 for first book & $1.25
for each additional book)
Outside US: $4.75 for first book
& $1.75 for each additional book)

SUBTOTAL_____

IN CANADA: ADD 7% GST_____

STATE TAX_____
(NY, OH & MN residents, please
add appropriate local sales tax)

FINAL TOTAL_____
(If paying in Canadian funds,
convert using the current
exchange rate. UNESCO
coupons welcome.)

☐ **BILL ME LATER:** ($5 service charge will be added)
(Bill-me option is good on US/Canada/Mexico orders only;
not good to jobbers, wholesalers, or subscription agencies.)

☐ Check here if billing address is different from
shipping address and attach purchase order and
billing address information.

Signature_____

☐ **PAYMENT ENCLOSED: $**_____

☐ **PLEASE CHARGE TO MY CREDIT CARD.**

☐ Visa ☐ MasterCard ☐ AmEx ☐ Discover
☐ Diners Club
Account #_____

Exp. Date_____

Signature_____

Prices in US dollars and subject to change without notice.

NAME_____

INSTITUTION_____

ADDRESS_____

CITY_____

STATE/ZIP_____

COUNTRY_____ COUNTY (NY residents only)_____

TEL_____ FAX_____

E-MAIL_____
May we use your e-mail address for confirmations and other types of information? ☐ Yes ☐ No

Order From Your Local Bookstore or Directly From
The Haworth Press, Inc.
10 Alice Street, Binghamton, New York 13904-1580 • USA
TELEPHONE: 1-800-HAWORTH (1-800-429-6784) / Outside US/Canada: (607) 722-5857
FAX: 1-800-895-0582 / Outside US/Canada: (607) 772-6362
E-mail: getinfo@haworth.com
PLEASE PHOTOCOPY THIS FORM FOR YOUR PERSONAL USE.

BOF96